UNDERST

SYSTEMS

UNDERSTANDING EXPERT SYSTEMS

Mike Van Horn
The Waite Group

BANTAM BOOKS
TORONTO · NEW YORK · LONDON · SYDNEY · AUCKLAND

UNDERSTANDING EXPERT SYSTEMS
A Bantam Book / March 1986

ISBN 0-553-34168-5

Published simultaneously in the United States and Canada

Bantam Books are published by Bantam Books, Inc. Its trade-
mark, consisting of the words "Bantam Books" and the por-
trayal of a rooster, is Registered in U.S. Patent and Trademark
Office and in other countries. Marca Registrada. Bantam
Books, Inc., 666 Fifth Avenue, New York, New York 10103.

PRINTED IN THE UNITED STATES OF AMERICA

B   0 9 8 7 6 5 4 3 2 1

*Dedicated with love to
my wife B.J.*

CONTENTS

Chapter 1   Expert on a Disk   1

Sherlock the computerized sleuth. What is an expert system? Why are these programs called expert systems? Some real expert systems. Mycin, the infectious disease expert. Prospector expert system finds $100,000,000 ore deposit. Expert systems: offspring of artificial intelligence. Panacea or peril? Bonanza or bust? Workhorse expert systems. Expert systems for all of us. What we will learn in this book. The ultimate personal expert.

Chapter 2   What Is an Expert System?   21

Why expert systems require knowledge. Conventional software uses "brute force" computing. The deadly "combinatorial explosion." How experts tackle problems. Heuristic problem-solving. What expert systems can do. Prospector's value. Solid conclusions in the face of uncertainty. Why Mycin is needed. R1 configures large computer systems. DEC relies on R1. Dendral predicts molecular structures of unknown compounds. Aircraft design—complex program but not an expert system. Common characteristics of expert system tasks.

Chapter 3   Developing a Small-Scale Expert System   55

Choosing the task for our expert system. The stock price predictor. Weather forecasting: a doable task? Starting a new expert system with examples. Improving your system's performance. How good can the system get? At its best, is the system worthwhile? Comparing the weather and stock price forecasters.

Chapter 4   Getting Knowledge into the Computer   76

Knowledge acquisition: how an expert system is created. Experts can't always explain how they solve problems. A knowledge engineer works with the experts. Stages in expert system development. Refining and upgrading the "post-graduate" expert system. The development of R1: a successful expert system. Two categories of rules: knowledge base and inference engine. Knowledge rules are separated from inferencing rules.

Chapter 5 Searching Through Knowledge for Answers   102
The forward reasoning treasure hunter. Dendral uses forward reasoning. The backward reasoning detective. Mycin uses backward reasoning. Why the different strategies? Chaining: reasoning by linking rules together. Forward chaining auto diagnosis. Strategies for efficient searching. The troubleshooter's inference engine. The system's limits. Backward-chaining Mycin-style diagnosis. High confidence from low confidence.

Chapter 6 How the Computer Reads Knowledge   127
What expert systems programs require. What makes Lisp a good expert systems language. Lisp compares apples and oranges. Lisp allows easy revisions. How Lisp allows backward chaining. How conceptual relationships are expressed. Propositional logic vs. predicate logic. How expert systems deal with uncertainty. Fuzzy sets. Natural language allows computer non-experts ease of use. How the computer understands what we say. Why is natural language so difficult for a computer?

Chapter 7 Developing Your Expert System   164
Unzipping one knowledge base and adding another. Early expert system shells and their descendants. The Mycin family—finding causes and prescribing cures. The R1 family—designing layouts and schedules. The Hearsay II family—recognizing patterns. Expert system development programs for microcomputers. Watch out for "Garbage in, gospel out."

Chapter 8 The Promise of Expert Systems   190
What expert systems are paying off now. When does it pay to develop expert systems? The problems and the promise of expert systems. What's right around the corner? Are expert systems intelligent, even artificially? Does an expert system learn? The social impact of expert systems.

References   223

Index   229

LIST OF KEY ILLUSTRATIONS, BOXES AND TABLES

	page
The Artificial Intelligence family tree	11
Contrasting Heuristics and Algorithms	29
The Expert System Branch of Artificial Intelligence with Recent Fruits	41
Common Characteristics of Expert System Tasks	48
Contrasting Characteristics of Conventional Software	49
What Tasks Are Expert Systems Right For?	53
Benefits of Expert Systems Compared to Human Experts	54
Checklist for Expert System Tasks	60
Principles for Building Expert Systems	74
Steps in Building an Expert System	85
Development Time and Man-years of Effort for Some Expert Systems	87
What Goes into the Expert System Program	97
When Backward and Forward Chaining Are Used	109
Comparing Forward and Backward Chaining	110
The Expert System, Focusing on the Inference Engine	116
Characteristics of Tasks and What Is Required of the Expert System	129
From Expert's Knowledge to Computer Language	144
How a Certainty Factor Is Calculated	145
Some of the Early Expert System Shells	181
Selected Expert System Development Programs	188

When Expert Systems Pay for Themselves   197

Barriers to the Development of Expert Systems   204

Converging Trends and the Boom in Expert Systems   206

Checklist for "Real" Expert Systems   216

The Knowledge Revolution Compared to the Automobile
Revolution   221

ACKNOWLEDGMENTS

I wish to thank all the people who helped bring this book to fruition. First, Judy Ziajka, my editor, who cajoled and encouraged and even tried to teach me the difference between "which" and "that." Next, all the people I worked with at the Waite Group: Robert Lafore, as good a model as any author could have, who helped me polish ideas and outline and simplify and organize and reorganize; Lyn Cordell for teaching me how a book is put together; Winston and Karen Sin for turning my flaky drawings and cartoons into real art; and Mitchell Waite for presenting me the opportunity to write the book. My thanks to Jono Hardjo and Jim Walsh at Bantam for their patience and for turning out a quality book. Many people shared ideas and material with me, especially Dan Shafer, Sue Spencer of Human Edge Software, Jeffrey Perrone on Expert-Ease, Ray Lauzzana, Dick Peddicord, Justin Millium, Jack Park, Kamran Parsaye, Ron Nakamoto, Michael Kleeman, Charles Seiter, David Coleman. Thanks also to Janet Perry and Paul Jensen for valuable editing feedback. In particular, I want to thank my father and mother for sending a steady stream of articles on all the latest developments in the field.

Most of all I wish to acknowledge my wife B.J. and daughter Becky, who put up with me during all the weekends and evenings spent writing. B.J., as a writer's wife, endured countless late night discussions about expert systems, then edited and entered all the revisions into the word processor. Truly we did it together.

PREFACE

Expert systems . . . a human expert's knowledge put onto a computer disk so that others can solve the same kind of problems. Will these latest fruits of artificial intelligence serve us well and transform the way we live and work, as some predict, or will they become our masters? "Human experts will be replaced as all expertise is put onto computer disks." "Every home and every car will have small expert systems as advisors and problem-solvers." "The claims are overblown: They aren't very expert and they're not intelligent."

These are the claims competing for your attention. How can you learn enough about these fascinating and mysterious products to make your own judgment?

You should read this book if you are curious about expert systems and artificial intelligence, and want to know what they do and how they work without having to master technical details. Basic notions, such as backward and forward reasoning, are illuminated using familiar parallels, such as treasure hunters, detectives, and auto troubleshooters. You will find out:

•How a human expert's intuitive rules of thumb get put into a computer so that it can solve problems otherwise beyond its capabilities.
•What the difference is between expert systems and conventional software.
•How good today's expert systems are, and how soon they will be practical for personal computers.
•How expert systems converse in natural language, but why it's so hard for a computer to understand plain English.

You will learn about current expert systems that diagnose deadly diseases, evaluate your loan application, and guide space shuttles to a safe landing—to see how they work and what situations justify their development.

Understanding Expert Systems offers you easy understanding of this rapidly emerging technology that promises to change the way we work and live and learn.

UNDERSTANDING EXPERT SYSTEMS

CHAPTER 1

EXPERT ON A DISK

A young girl is missing and the police are baffled. Is it a kidnapping or a runaway? Her parents are frantic, absolutely sure their daughter has met with foul play. But the police are not so sure. To them, this is just like so many other frustrating cases: The clues are skimpy and confusing, and there's a good chance the girl is a runaway who doesn't want to be found. Their dilemma is whether to spend countless hours searching for leads on a girl who turns out to be a runaway, or to put the case on the back burner with other runaway cases and thus risk injury or death to a kidnap victim.

The tragedy is that most of the information needed to solve this case rapidly already exists, but it is scattered through the records and files of police departments across the country and in pychologists' minds. Police psychologists can put together profiles of kidnappers and how they operate; police and FBI records scattered throughout the country contain data on the modus operandi of known kidnappers, and new information gets fed into these unconnected databases every day. If only all these experts could get together and pool their knowledge and information, this case could be rapidly solved. We want this girl back, so let's magically combine all these resources into Sherlock 9000, the computerized sleuth. Sherlock is a computer program that can draw upon all these databases, including the psychological profiles of kidnappers, and thus aid the police in solving the case. Let's see it go into action.

Sergeant Sanchez sits down at his computer terminal in his Los Angeles office and plugs into our computerized expert, Sherlock. As

Sherlock flashes questions on the screen, he types in the kind of case he has before him and the known facts:

```
Please select type of case:
1-Bank Robbery
2-Hostages held
3-Kidnapping
4-Missing child
5-Skyjacking
6-Terrorist
```

Sherlock can tackle several different types of crimes. It has expert knowledge built into it from the foremost crimebusters for each type of crime. They have painstakingly explained how they cracked their cases: what clues they looked for, how they interpreted these clues, and how they tied pieces together to find matches among disparate data. In essence, using Sherlock is like having a super advisor at our fingertips. But this advisor needs our guidance and input to be able to give us worthwhile opinions. This particular expert system asks you lots of questions to help it zero in on the solution.

Since Sergeant Sanchez is not sure whether this crime is a kidnapping, he enters "4" for "Missing child." Sherlock will now ask questions to find out whether this case looks like a runaway or a kidnapping. Like any good detective, Sherlock must first gather all the facts of the case. As Sherlock flashes questions on the computer screen, Sergeant Sanchez types in the answers: When and where was the girl last seen? What was she wearing? What was her behavior before she disappeared? Did anything out of the ordinary happen? Did she have any fights with her parents? Was she having trouble in school? Were any strange people or cars seen in the vicinity of where she disappeared? There are many more questions. Sherlock usually understands Sergeant Sanchez's "natural language" responses, and if it doesn't understand, it asks Sanchez to clarify or elaborate.

The sergeant, however, is not used to using this system, and some of Sherlock's questions don't make sense to him. So he occasionally asks Sherlock:

```
Why?
```

That is, Sergeant Sanchez is asking Sherlock why the computer is asking certain questions. Sherlock obliges by answering:

```
I am trying to establish whether this is
a kidnapping or a runaway.
```

To many of the questions Sherlock asks, the sergeant has to answer "Not known." Sherlock reviews all the input so far and automatically checks to see what additional input it needs to reach a reliable conclusion. It then says:

```
I will need answers to these questions to
reach a conclusion.
```

Sherlock then lists several key questions that Sergeant Sanchez couldn't answer. The sergeant has to go back and reinterview the missing girl's family, friends, schoolmates, and neighbors to get the needed information, and naturally everything they say is fragmentary, inconsistent, and incomplete. But when Sanchez returns and enters this new information into Sherlock, it turns out to be sufficient for Sherlock, which states:

```
I conclude with confidence of .70 that
subject was kidnapped. There is a
likelihood of .25 that subject is a
runaway.
```

Sherlock is 70 percent sure that the child was kidnapped. This is like our weather forecaster saying, "There is a 70 percent chance of rain tomorrow." Sherlock has combined many small pieces of information, some of which are uncertain or seemingly conflicting, and reached a conclusion. Of course, this is just the way a human expert sleuth works.

This is just the first step, but it is enough to mobilize nationwide information resources. Sherlock now builds a profile of this kidnapping, using many small bits of information culled from interviews and observations, and compares this to the modus operandi of known or suspected kidnappers and child molesters. This profile is transmitted to police computers and national data centers to see if it matches profiles built from other cases. Sherlock finds several low-likelihood matches, and the police check them out, but to no avail. The most likely suspect is a man who is in prison for a similar kidnapping.

During the next several weeks, new local data is periodically fed into the various data systems. Sergeant Sanchez instructs Sherlock to scan it. A seemingly routine report of a parole violation brings Sherlock into action. The suspect who had been in prison was released on parole, but it had taken a while for this information to be put into the system where Sherlock could spot it.

Alerted by Sherlock, the police quickly trace the suspect to his old neighborhood in Phoenix. They find the girl, locked in a house but safe. She and her parents are happily reunited. Sherlock does it again!

WHAT IS AN EXPERT SYSTEM?

Sherlock would be a wonderful piece of software, wouldn't it? Although it is still a dream, it is quite similar to other computer programs called expert systems that have been developed in recent years. An expert system is a brand-new breed of commercial software program that is based on the ideas of artificial intelligence. Until recently, artificial intelligence systems required huge computers and performed esoteric tasks. But this is rapidly changing. Expert systems are emerging that can run on personal computers, and these systems are likely to have a profound impact on the ways we work and live.

So "expert system" is now one of the latest computer buzzwords. But just what do expert systems do and how do they differ from other types of software? Many articles and books discuss expert systems. Yet most offer few details about how they work; and books that provide some detail seem aimed at computer professionals. In this book, we will strike a middle course. We will see what expert systems do, how they work, and how they differ from other computer programs. We will also see some real expert systems in action. Throughout this book, we will see how expert systems are maturing and evolving from programs that once ran only on large, expensive computers into programs that run on low-cost microcomputers.

WHY ARE THESE PROGRAMS CALLED EXPERT SYSTEMS?

Expert systems programs emulate the problem-solving processes of human experts. Expert systems actually have built into them the knowledge of human experts, and they draw on it to solve problems. As we will see in Chapter 2, this differs markedly from conventional computer programs, which manipulate numbers and quantities, pluses and minuses, in precisely specified ways. Most important, this ability to emulate human thought processes allows expert systems to tackle tasks previously beyond the reach of computers. What we will here call expert systems, many others label as knowledge-based systems, or rule-based systems, or knowledge enhancers. Some people make distinctions among these, but we will lump them all together as expert systems.

For an expert system to be developed in the first place, human experts must work closely with a new kind of professional—a "knowledge engineer"—who knows how to tease out the experts' knowledge and ways of solving problems, even when the experts themselves aren't aware of them, and to encode this in a form the computer can use. We will show that interaction in Chapter 4.

SOME REAL EXPERT SYSTEMS

Two actual expert systems programs, built over the last decade or so and in use long enough for us to have solid refined bodies of knowledge about them, are Mycin and Prospector. Looking at them will give us a feel for what is true today.

Mycin, the Infectious Disease Expert

At the Stanford Medical Center, a young man lies barely conscious, bathed in the sweat of a high fever. He entered the hospital several days ago for minor surgery and had been recovering nicely. Then, suddenly, a fever developed. His physician, Dr. Lee, quickly took new blood tests and carefully observed his symptoms, but she

Figure 1–1
During an expert system session, the user types responses to
questions flashed on the computer screen by the expert system, which is actually a computer program stored on a disk.

realized she wouldn't have time to wait for results from all of the blood
tests—some cultures would take several days to develop. Furthermore, the symptoms she observed weren't at all what she had expected to see. Dr. Lee will have to go forward with only partial
information and good guesses. She decided she had better call in the
expert.

The "expert" is Mycin, a real expert system designed to help
medical specialists diagnose infectious blood diseases, then prescribe
the proper antibiotics for them. Mycin's name, in fact, comes from
the suffix of many common antibiotics. Let's watch the doctor work with
Mycin. Dr. Lee brings the results of the patient's tests and her

notes from her observations and sits down to type at the computer keyboard. As Mycin flashes questions on its screen, she types in the answers. Mycin tells Dr. Lee:

```
Please enter the results of positive
cultures.
```

The doctor types in the names of the microorganisms found during the tests. Mycin responds:

```
Please enter the results of the negative
cultures.
```

The doctor enters the names of organisms that could have been in the samples, but which were not found. It is just as important to know what is not present as what is present.

Mycin concludes that the organisms found in the blood smears and urine and sputum samples don't account for the observed symptoms. Another line of questioning is pursued. Mycin asks:

```
Has patient recently had symptoms of
persistent headache or other abnormal
neurological symptoms (dizziness,
lethargy, etc.)?
```

Dr. Lee responds:

```
YES.
```

Mycin:

```
Has patient had objective evidence of
abnormal neurologic signs (coma, seizures,
rigidity)?
```

Doctor:

```
YES
```

Mycin:

```
Then the cultures will be considered to
be associated with MENINGITIS.
```

Meningitis? That's a surprise. But what is the source? Meningitis can be caused by a number of bacterial organisms. Mycin asks a series of other questions about the patient's appearance, symptoms, and history. Then Mycin asks:

```
Is this meningitis a hospital-acquired
infection?
```

The doctor is surprised at Mycin's question and asks why it is important to determine whether the infection was acquired while the patient was hospitalized.

Mycin is not trying to suggest that hospital conditions are unclean. It informs the doctor:

```
This data will aid in determining the
organisms (other than those seen on
cultures or smears) that might be causing
the infection.
```

After the doctor answers several more questions, Mycin summarizes:

```
I have found evidence that treatment
should cover for E. coli causing
meningitis.
```

Mycin lists the organisms that are most likely to be causing the meningitis and then asks further questions to determine the appropriate treatment. Mycin explains its prescriptions:

```
My therapy recommendations will be
designed to treat for organisms that
either are very likely or, although less
likely, would have a significant effect
on therapy selection if they were present.
```

Finally, Mycin prints the best antibiotic therapy to maximize the chances of effective coverage of the cause of the infection while keeping the number, toxicity, and side effects of drugs to a minimum.

Dr. Lee is not satisfied, however, and asks Mycin to display the next choice therapy. Mycin prints this, along with a comparison of the two treatments. From this output, Dr. Lee is able to select the best combination of antibiotics for this particular patient and his infection, and is able to do it quickly. Using Mycin is like having the top experts in the field at her disposal. Mycin may well have saved the life of this patient by spotting this unexpected but rapidly-developing meningitis infection. It did this by examining incomplete and preliminary data, long before conclusive test results were available.

Since 1979, Mycin has been used innumerable times at the Stanford Medical Center, and its results rival those of the top experts in the field. It also has spawned several related systems, including Oncocin, which helps diagnose cancer, and Puff, which diagnoses pulmonary disorders. Mycin was a pioneering expert system, and it took years of painstaking work to make it operational. Mycin can perform many tasks that are beyond the reach of conventional software.

For example, Mycin contains the expertise of some of the foremost experts in the field of infectious blood diseases. It uses this expertise to guide its operators to the most reasonable conclusions and then recommends the best alternative treatments for the problems it diagnoses. Using Mycin means that the expertise of the best minds in the field can be called upon twenty-four hours any day from anywhere in the world.

Mycin can also sift through a mountain of data and not forget to ask a single significant question, unlike even the best doctor caught in the heat of the moment. It reaches a solid conclusion even with input that is incomplete and uncertain. When it lacks any information needed to reach a conclusion, it asks its operator for it.

Mycin communicates in English, not computerese. This is essential, since Mycin's users are doctors, not computer experts. Mycin structures its questions and explanations in English and understands the doctor's "natural language" responses. True, its communication is limited to a narrow range of technical jargon, but this is generally the way physicians communicate in such circumstances, anyway.

Mycin explains why it reaches the conclusions it does. This also is essential because doctors using Mycin are facing life-and-death situations, and they need to be able to check Mycin's recommendations against their own expertise.

Mycin could well be called the grandmother of expert systems. Many of the basic principles of expert systems that we will explore in this book were worked out during Mycin's development. As you can see in figure 2–1, "An Expert System Family Tree," in Chapter 2, Mycin is the parent of several generations of successful expert systems, including programs that can be used to develop other expert systems. The people developing today's easy-to-use microcomputer-sized expert systems all stand on the shoulders of Mycin.

Let's now turn to another pioneering expert system, Prospector, which could be called a nephew of Mycin.

Prospector Expert System Finds $100,000,000 Ore Deposit

Here are three views of the same land:

—A noisy old four-engine plane flies low over the bleak foothills of central Washington state, making repeated passes over a carefully selected area. On each wingtip, magnetometers and other instruments continually scan the ground. The signals received are recorded on large reels of magnetic tape.

—From its orbit 380 miles up in space, Landsat surveys the same terrain and maps it in meticulous detail, sending back to earth detailed data on the likely mineral resources under each acre.

—Later, geologists with jeeps and packmules crisscross the area, drilling core samples of earth and carefully noting rock formations.

What can we do with these different views? Prospector, another expert system, can digest and evaluate these kinds of data when they are fed into it by a trained geologist, and use the information to pinpoint likely locations for valuable ore deposits. It has found a molybdenum deposit worth $100,000,000. Where was Prospector when it made this discovery? At SRI International, a research institute near San Francisco, 1500 miles from where the deposit was later verified.

EXPERT SYSTEMS: OFFSPRING OF ARTIFICIAL INTELLIGENCE

The expert system is the most practical application to date of a branch of computer science which fascinates and mystifies many of us: artificial intelligence, or "AI." AI researchers try to develop computer programs that emulate the way people use their minds to tackle

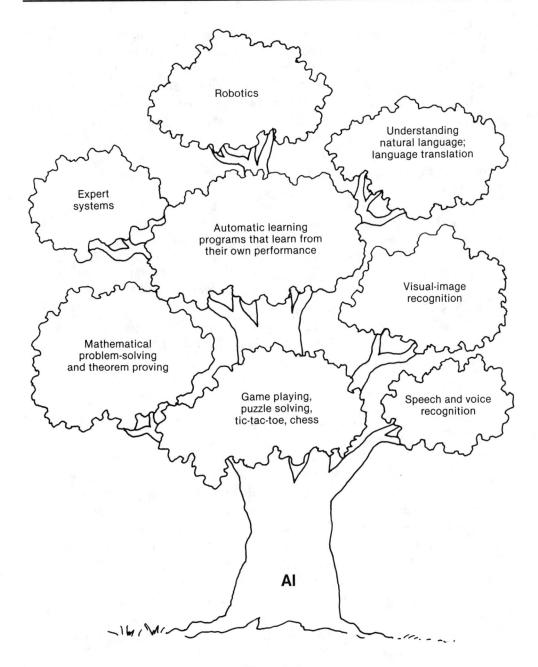

Figure 1–2
The Artificial Intelligence family tree

problems beyond the reach of "ordinary" computers. Figure 1–2, "AI Family Tree," shows the main topics investigated by AI researchers.

From its beginnings in the late 1950s, AI has inspired dreams and nightmares of computers and robots excelling humans at virtually every important task. Experience, however, has been humbling to these visionaries. AI researchers quickly discovered just how difficult it is to program a computer to understand speech as well as a five-year-old can, or play chess as well as a junior high school student can, or operate an image recognition system that can spot a truck from an airplane.

Even though AI is still largely confined to the research laboratory, practical applications are emerging more and more rapidly. We still don't have household robots to clean our houses and bring us breakfast in bed, but industrial robots on assembly lines are bringing us cheaper and better products and displacing workers. HAL 9000 of *2001: A Space Odyssey* fame is still a distant fantasy, but we do have computers that respond to spoken commands.

And now we also have expert systems. Expert systems is one area of artificial intelligence that has climbed down from the ivory tower, rolled up its sleeves, and gone to work.

EXPERT SYSTEMS: PANACEA OR PERIL?

Systems like Mycin, Prospector, and Sherlock look like unmitigated blessings, right? Mycin could make available to every medical center the diagnostic skill of the best doctors in the field. The general approach used in Mycin can be adapted to create diagnostic systems for many other diseases. The expertise in these systems can be supplemented and refined through experience, so that soon they could excel any expert. Millions of lives could be saved.

Or Prospector could cull the warehouses full of Landsat data already gathered and sift it for likely deposits of oil, precious metals, or underground water reservoirs. If Prospector could eliminate 99 percent of unlikely sites, and highlight only the best prospects, it would pay for itself many times over.

As both mainframe and microcomputer expert systems proliferate, these things are coming to pass. Yet some people dread the

widespread application of expertise by computers to such problems. They fear its misuse. Consider this press release of the future:

TaxMax Socks Lax Taxpayers

The Internal Revenue Service today unveiled TaxMax, its new expert system program designed to identify likely tax cheats even before they commit an offense. The IRS has built profiles of those people most likely to evade taxes. Its knowledge base includes the data in all national credit agencies. It feeds this into a set of models of personal behavior, which correlates a family's spending and credit habits with its likelihood to understate taxes due. TaxMax will review data on all taxpayers and flag names that score above a certain threshold. The IRS will then target these people for annual audits for the next five years.

Today's TaxMax Is Here

Does this seem farfetched? Consider a system already available. Here is advice excerpted from the Sales Edge, a program available for $250 for an IBM PC. Using salespeople's answers to eighty-six questions about themselves and their sales prospects, Sales Edge tells them:

—How to approach Mr. M, the sales prospect: "Take care to open with a neutral posture, since you normally tend to be competitive and aggressive, a stance that could bring out Mr. M's defensiveness."

—How to present information. "Be aware that you tend to focus on the 'big picture,' while Mr. M is very concerned with details."

—How to close with Mr. M: "Mr. M gets very anxious when pressed to make a big decision, so concentrate on one detail at a time to relax him."

The Sales Edge has built into it the same kind of behavior profiles that we postulated for TaxMax, though psychologists question whether it is possible to construct an accurate and useful behavior profile from eighty-six factors. If we base our selling strategy to Mr. M on the profile we get from Sales Edge, and it is inaccurate, we may fail to make the sale.

One of the biggest dangers with the use of expert systems is that poorly trained users may let the expert system make their decisions for them instead of using the system as an advisor. We could call this the "garbage in, gospel out" syndrome. Let's look at one case of this.

Loan officers in commercial lending institutions are using expert systems that advise them whether or not to grant credit. Suppose Samuel Ness, president of LoTech, applies for an expansion of the line of credit for his company. His banker types this query like this into his computer:

```
LoTech, Inc. current credit situation?
```

Prompted by this request, the computer displays this data:

```
LoTech's existing line of credit is
$2,500,000. LoTech's interest rate is
prime plus 1.5. LoTech has not missed any
loan payments.
```

The banker then types in:

```
Should this loan be approved?
```

The machine responds:

```
No.
```

When asked the reasons for the denial, the computer says:

```
LoTech supplies peripheral devices to
Banana Computers, HotStuff Technologies,
and Diehard Disk Drives. These three
companies, although showing strong sales,
have shown poor earnings and may have
cash problems. Thus, LoTech's receivables
may turn into bad debts. Extension of a
loan at this time is ill-advised.
```

The president of LoTech may feel that there are important factors that the computer just didn't take into consideration. But the junior loan officer is taking Loan Arranger's advice as final. He feels that the people whose knowledge went into this software know a lot more than he does, and so he does not feel competent to question their decision.

But let's look at the positive side. If profiles are constructed carefully, they can provide us with invaluable advice, even if it is negative. Suppose Mr. Ness's banker has tipped him off to a potentially dangerous situation with his main customers, a situation of which he wasn't aware. He can now take steps to correct it.

But if computers start making our decisions about love, money, and good old competition, what is left for us humans? Before we get too excited or alarmed by all that expert systems promise, let's look more closely at current reality.

Expert Systems: Bonanza or Bust?

Most of the criticism expert systems receive comes not from those who fear they will take over the world but from the doubters. Many knowledgeable computer commentators predict expert systems will never live up to their promise. Neither Mycin nor Prospector, for example, are in active service. They are used only for training and research. People question whether Prospector really discovered the molybdenum deposit, or whether the system was led so close to a likely deposit that it couldn't miss. Mycin's team of dedicated specialists, who developed and nurtured the program, has disbanded. At present, these systems seem too expensive to maintain.

Many computer scientists who worked on these large computer expert systems scoff at claims for the systems available for personal computers. These are really not expert systems, they say, maintaining that they are based on inadequate pop psychology models. Although there is some truth to this, it is undeniable that software for the vast personal computer market is moving into areas that were once the exclusive realm of expensive mainframes. As microcomputer-based programs become ever more powerful, expert system counterparts to "Wordstar" or "Lotus 1–2–3" will be developed.

Workhorse Expert Systems

Although it is true that some of the claims made for expert systems are overblown, some programs have been solid successes, and more are on the way. Here are several expert systems that pay their own way in everyday use:

—R1 is used by Digital Equipment Corporation (DEC) to find the best layout and part configuration for the VAX minicomputer systems it sells, given each customer's situation and hardware needs. It contains the knowledge from hundreds of skilled DEC technicians who have set up systems and worked with R1 since 1979. It can now lay out any VAX system better than the best technician, and DEC relies heavily on it.

    —Dendral, developed by Nobel Prize winner Joshua Lederberg at Stanford, is used daily by chemists all over the country to discover the molecular structure of unknown organic compounds.

    —Delta/Cats was built by General Electric to troubleshoot malfunctions in diesel locomotive engines.

    —Sophie trains electronics engineering students at the Massachusetts Institute of Technology (MIT) to design and troubleshoot electronic circuits.

    —ISIS, developed by Carnegie-Mellon University, is used by Westinghouse to schedule the most efficient use of its job shop and to manage its job shop projects.

    As we can see from the examples presented thus far, the proven expert systems are used in large industrial or institutional settings for tasks that are generally remote to our lives. Why should we be excited about these tools, then, unless we are computer experts or production managers?

EXPERT SYSTEMS FOR ALL OF US

    In the past, expert systems have been limited to larger and more expensive computers because of the large amount of memory required to hold the expert's knowledge, which takes far more memory space than does the numerical data of conventional software. But the memory available for smaller computers is increasing exponentially, and prices for computing power are plummeting. Thus, what could only be done on a VAX minicomputer a few years ago will soon be possible on an IBM PC or Apple Macintosh.

    And, of course, we have learned a lot from previous efforts. The pioneering expert systems took years to develop and required the skills of the best experts in the field and the generous funding of universities and research institutes. But the territory they carved out is now open to the settlers. Many prognosticators assure us that within a few years expert systems on a floppy disk selling for $49.95 will be available to advise us on every conceivable task.

In addition to Sales Edge, mentioned earlier, other expert system programs are already on the market:

—Negotiation Edge helps us get what we want in any negotiation, by assessing profiles of the people negotiating.

—Management Edge advises us on how to improve our management styles, using information we give it about ourselves.

—Relationship Edge advises us on how to resolve problems with our spouses, lovers, children, employees, goldfish, and in-laws.

—A program for PCs allows us to diagnose our own medical symptoms at home. Perhaps it should be called Hypochondriac's Edge. Fortunately, it tells us when to go directly to the doctor.

And even more exciting, we can also buy software that will guide us in building our own customized expert systems in any areas in which we have enough expertise—and patience. People have already built personal expert systems to help them do everything from select the right wine to plan an investment portfolio. But remember the "garbage in, gospel out" syndrome. We'll explore these customized expert systems in Chapter 3.

What We Will Learn Here

Expert systems, these fascinating but mysterious programs, are bursting into our consciousness with the force of the latest rock superstar. Much of what is written about them is steeped in technical details and jargon, or is full of unexplained generalities.

In this book, we will see how a contraption of metal, silicon chips, and spinning plastic disks can assimilate an expert's knowledge and solve problems in a complex field at least as well as the top people in that field. We won't learn how to build an expert system. But we will answer your questions about what makes these things tick, using many diagrams and concrete examples from actual expert systems. We will answer questions like these:

—Why aren't Sherlock and TaxMax already operational? Why has it been so difficult to make expert systems practical and cost effective, and what developments will change this? What kinds of jobs do expert systems do well, and what jobs do they do poorly?

—How do expert system programs differ from any other kind of software program? How do they reason and draw on an expert's knowledge and come to conclusions? How does this expertise get into the machine in the first place, and how is it refined and improved once it is there?

—What results have expert systems produced? What can they do that a human expert cannot? What can these systems do for you and me?

—What promise and hazards do expert systems hold for our society? Will programs like TaxMax destroy the last vestiges of our privacy? Will too much power be concentrated in the hands of those who can afford such systems? Will we destroy ourselves by turning over life-and-death decisions to computerized experts? Will human intelligence be rendered obsolete?

The Ultimate Personal Expert

But now, before we move on to these weighty issues, let's indulge in one more scenario. Let's introduce:

ESTHER—Expert System to Help Establish Relationships

Esther helps you find a date or a mate. She lives in a small portable computer you can easily carry in your briefcase or purse. You talk with Esther and she talks back. You tell Esther what kind of person you are looking for, and she will advise you on finding her or him. Esther's expertise has been built up from interviews with scores of successful swingers.

Esther listens in on conversations between you and the person you are pursuing. She analyzes what she hears, according to her models of behavior and what she knows about you. After a while, you should take her aside. She will ask you some important questions: What is this person wearing? drinking? What is his or her astrological sign? Then she will give you a strategy for getting together with this person. Or she may tell you, "Stay away!" If you are pursuing several people, she will help you rank them by desirability. She will also tell you how much you are likely to have to spend on a date with each person.

But that's not all! Take Esther along on your first date and she will alert you with a discreet beep when propositions you don't want to deal with are coming up, or when you are approaching your preset spending limit. When you hear Esther's warning signal, you can pretend it is your belt beeper, and excuse yourself, saying, "I must go to the phone." When Esther has told you what the impending problem is, if you want to cut things short, you can return and say, "Sorry, I'm going to have to leave. It's an emergency."

Esther won't nag, and she won't get jealous. Interested? Just send a check for $99.95 plus postage and handling with your order form to . . .

CHAPTER 2

WHAT IS AN EXPERT SYSTEM?

- **Why Expert Systems Require Knowledge**
- **Heuristic vs. Logical Problem-Solving**
- **What Expert Systems Can Do**
- **How They Differ from Conventional Software**

What does the "expert" in "expert system" refer to? As we said in Chapter 1, it refers to the fact that an expert system has human experts' knowledge programmed into it in such a way that it can tackle problems previously beyond the reach of a computer.

"But surely," you ask, "doesn't it take a lot of expertise to build any computer software program?" Of course it does. Any "conventional" software program, such as an accounting program, a database program, or a program to computer the orbits of satellites, is the product of just as much expertise as any expert system. But an expert system contains specialized expertise in a different form from other software, and it uses that expertise differently to reach a conclusion. We're going to show you what this difference is and why it is important.

In this chapter, we'll see why an expert system must be based upon built-in knowledge, by seeing how an expert tackles problems. We will then show you four mainframe-based expert systems, to give you a concrete idea of what they do, and what kind of knowledge they contain. Then we will contrast expert systems to conventional software, and finish the chapter by showing what kind of tasks expert systems are good for and not so good for.

WHY EXPERT SYSTEMS REQUIRE KNOWLEDGE

Conventional Software Uses "Brute Force" Computing

To understand why expert systems programs require built-in knowledge, you must know why conventional software does not. We'll define "conventional software" as a software program that relies on computational power alone to reach a solution. Above, we gave as one example a financial accounting program. Let's take a simplified statement which would be programmed into any typical accounting program:

Sales Revenue
–Cost of Goods Sold
–General and Administrative Expenses
= Net profit Before Taxes

This is an example of a computer "algorithm," a precisely-stated formula upon which a computer program is based. There are several things immediately apparent about this equation. Each factor is precisely defined, and the definitions are all stated in terms of numbers and numerical relationships. There is widespread agreement among the accounting experts about these definitions, and they don't change much over time. Any accounting program follows a rigid series of steps to reach the bottom line. All the data fed into it must be numerical, and if any piece is missing, a conclusion cannot be reached. For any particular set of circumstances there will be one best answer. When you get it, you know it. All this is equally true for even a very complex computation of a space shuttle's orbit, which may require a supercomputer.

This "number-crunching" approach works wonderfully well and fast, and has led to the computer revolution of the last several decades. In fact, advances were made so rapidly for a while that computer gurus rashly predicted that before long computers would be able to surpass human intelligence, just by reducing everything to numbers and processing them faster and ever faster. But they ran into a stone wall because many of the most interesting problems just couldn't be reduced to numbers. And these were the kinds of problems—like finding good mining sites or telling what illness someone has—at which not only experts, but even ordinary mortals, could beat the socks off the fastest computers.

The Deadly "Combinatorial Explosion"

Well, why can't these interesting problems be reduced to numbers? Why isn't it just a matter of building large enough computers? Interestingly enough, humans seem to be able to recognize paths to solutions in a way that computers do not. (For example, any person trying to fix a car that won't start doesn't worry about whether the windows roll down or not.) Scientists are able to find the most probable areas for research from among a large range of possibilities. If we could not do this, the number of possibilities to be checked out would overwhelm us and nothing would be done. The way possibilities pile up is called the "combinatorial explosion"; like many explosions, this one proved deadly to some early expert systems.

Let's look for a moment to one of the earliest areas researched by people experimenting with artificial intelligence—game playing. Games provided small manageable problems with clear objectives and stated rules. Chess became a popular subject for experiments because it was a complex and highly abstract game.

Early attempts to develop a chess playing program were based strictly on a computational method. Programmers tried to develop a set of formulas, or algorithms, that would specify each possible move throughout the entire game, taking into consideration every possible move your opponent could make at each turn, and then define rules based on a scoring method that would select the single best move at each turn.

In principle, it would be possible to write such a set of rules. There are no unexplored corners of the chess board, and no new rules are likely to be invented for the game. However, this would take a *very* large number of rules, even if limitations were programmed in, such as considering only those moves that improve your position.

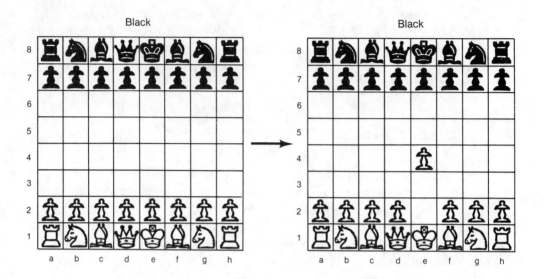

Consider the sixteen chess pieces with which each player starts the game. Think of the number of possible moves you have on your first turn, then each possible move your opponent might make, then each possible move you might make, and so on. How many would there be? We must discover the number of possible moves in each turn, and multiply them all together.

Turn #	No. of possible moves
1. You	20
1. Opponent	x20
Turn 1 = 20 × 20 = 400	
2. You	× 12 (We'll be conservative, and consider
2. Opponent	× 12 only "feasible" moves.)
After Turn 2 = 57,600	
. . .	× . . .
. . .	× . . .

If more than 50,000 rules would be required to specify all the possible moves for just the first two turns, you can see how rapidly the number of rules would multiply with each turn. For a typical game, the number would be beyond astronomical.

```
  . . .           × . . .
  . . .           × . . .
"Checkmate!"      = 10^120 possible board positions.
                  (That is: 1 followed by 120 zeroes.)
```

"Checkmate!" $= 10^{120}$ possible board positions. (That is: 1 followed by 120 zeroes.)

This demonstrates a "combinatorial explosion," so-called because when you combine all the possibilities you must program into your number crunching program, the number quickly explodes! It has been calculated that if all the fastest supercomputers worked constantly on computing every possible chess move, they couldn't finish the job by the time the universe ended. So it quickly became apparent that any game-playing program based on calculation could compete with humans only on very simple problems, like Tic-Tac-Toe, in which sheer rapid computational power is paramount.

How is it that any sixth-grade kid with a plastic chess board can outperform all the assembled supercomputers so easily? He learns a few rules and tricks to improve his game, and develops strategy. People developing chess playing programs quickly started incorporating chess strategy rules: shortcuts, ways to evaluate what your opponent is likely to do if you make a particular move, ways to shift your strategy as the game develops.

What they did was to program in knowledge. And where does this knowledge come from? From a chess expert. And it is no easy task to get the chess expert to be able to explain clearly, concisely, and systematically how he forms strategies and evaluates possible moves several turns ahead.

Successful chess programmers, like successful chess players, combine strategical and tactical thinking to decide on moves. Tactical thinking uses the basic rules of the game to proceed along specified lines; a chess program does this when it evaluates all possible moves from a position. Strategic thinking uses shortcuts, psychology, and rules of thumb to decide between possible moves. Attempts to program strategic thinking into computers is at the heart of expert systems, and it is so difficult that there have never been successful programs written for games like Go, which are almost entirely strategic.

Now chess, as complex as it is, is simple compared to medical diagnosis or prospecting. The problem domain for chess can be completely defined, every possible move is known, rules are set, and winning strategies are widely agreed upon. If chess programs require

knowledge and strategic thinking, you can imagine the level of sophisticated programming these other problems must require. That is why,
for a long time, only people who had the knowledge could successfully
attack them. The experts in artificial intelligence began designing
expert systems by studying the ways that human experts gain information about these problems, and the rules they use to make expert
decisions about them.

How Experts Tackle Problems

Back in the dark ages before computerized expert systems, we
relied on human experts to handle problems like the ones described in
Chapter 1. Why do humans—both experts and mere mortals—excel at
solving complex problems? We don't rely on our general problem-
solving skills very much, but on the knowledge we have about the
situation. We solve tough problems by breaking them down into
smaller pieces, and by seeking patterns in the data which seem promising or meaningful to pursue. We quickly prune the problem down by
rejecting unlikely outcomes. We often combine results from several
lines of inquiry. We look for an answer that is "good enough" or that
seems likely, then we test it. We make educated guesses when necessary.

We bring to bear all our knowledge on the problem. Our knowledge includes not only "book learning," or the facts that are commonly
known, but also all our personal, tacit knowledge built up over our
lifetimes from experience with similar situations. Our hunches, intu-
itions, and sudden flashes of insight come from this tacit knowledge,
much of which we are not even aware we have.

For example, suppose you try to start your car in the morning.
The engine turns over, but it won't start. Now you could immediately
begin going through a predetermined troubleshooting routine, checking every item on a list of things that can go wrong. But this could take
all day. So you immediately kick in your vast diagnostic expertise. You
know that since the engine turns over, your battery isn't dead. Since
the gas gauge reads half-full, you presume you are not out of gas. Since
you can now smell gasoline, you must have flooded it by pumping the
accelerator, and this at least means that the engine is getting gas. You
check under the hood, and find no obvious loose wires. You notice that

it is an unusually cold, damp morning, so you suspect that the dampness may have affected the points or spark plugs. And so on until you either isolate the problem, or decide it is beyond your diagnostic skill and call AAA.

But in either case, you first check the most likely causes of trouble and quickly eliminate items. You seek indirect indicators of trouble or lack of trouble. You take the most likely option. For example, the gas gauge might be broken, but you tacitly decide that this is unlikely. To do all this diagnosing, you rely on your long experience with balky cars.

Our ability to solve problems in this way is what we call our intelligence. And of course experts solve problems in exactly the same way. They may call upon more book learning than we do, but their seat-of-the-pants experience may well prove decisive.

Heuristic Problem-Solving

So you see that many experts don't use a rigorous, systematic approach to solving problems in their field. Instead, they use a "heuristic" approach. "Heuristic" describes a central concept for expert systems. A heuristic is a "rule of thumb" used to solve problems. It hasn't been rigorously proven—it probably can't be—but through experience has proven to be a useful and reliable guide to action. "Heuristic" comes from the same Greek word as "Eureka!" which means "I found it!" This corresponds to the "Aha!" feeling we have when we suddenly find the answer to a nagging problem.

In many ways, the unproven but useful "heuristic" contrasts with the formal "algorithm" we described above, even though it is actually a type of algorithm. Everyone uses both heuristics and algorithms. Here are some everyday examples of heuristics:

"When the stock market hits a high, it will probably go down the next day due to profit-taking."

"If it is third down with long yardage, the offense will probably pass."

**"Red skies at night,
shepherds delight;**

**Red skies in the morning,
shepherds take warning."**

**"If a horse enters a man's house and bites either an ass or a
man, the owner of the house will die and his household will be
scattered."**

(from an ancient Babylonian tablet)

Notice that all of these heuristic statements have the same form, which
goes like this:

If a certain situation occurs, *then* a known outcome is likely;
and we can know its likelihood at least tacitly, and this
outcome points to an appropriate action we should take.

This *if . . . then* statement is the bedrock of expert systems. You will
see knowledge stated in this form throughout this book.

You can see why using heuristics is often called "the art of
good guessing." Heuristic rules allow experts to solve problems
much more rapidly. And many problems just cannot be solved without
using a heuristic knowledge-based approach. It is the heuristic
knowledge of experts that must be captured for an expert system.
Computer experts soon saw that standard number-crunching and
general problem-solving methods wouldn't work on many tough problems. They saw that to obtain results which would rival an expert's
performance, they would have to simulate the expert's heuristic
problem-solving approaches, and apply these to the expert's conceptual
knowledge.

Thus was born the field of expert systems. This is one of the
central premises of artificial intelligence: harness the approaches of
intelligent problem-solvers to crack tough problems. Easier said than
done, as we will see in the next several chapters.

WHAT EXPERT SYSTEMS CAN DO

Armed with our new knowledge of heuristic problem-solving, let's
turn again to see what some well-known expert systems do and what
kind of knowledge they contain. We'll describe four different kinds of

CONTRASTING HEURISTICS AND ALGORITHMS

HEURISTICS	ALGORITHMS
If it ain't broke, don't fix it.	$1 + 2 = 3$
The lower the price/earnings ratio the better buy a stock is likely to be.	The price/earnings ratio equals the stock's market price divided by the firm's latest retained earnings per share.
Select moves which protect the center of the chess board.	Black pawn at square D7, and square D6 and square D5 are empty, move pawn from D7 to D5.
If the car engine doesn't turn over when you turn the key, first check for loose wires, then for a dead battery.	
These are rules of thumb, proven generally reliable through experience, but not always correct. They are concepts, and can't be reduced to numbers.	These are exactly stated formulas which can be logically proven. Put in correct numerical data and you will get the correct answer.

expert systems, which illustrate the four most common approaches. These are "pioneering" expert systems, built for use on large mainframe computers. They are unlike the ones for mini- or microcomputers that you are most likely to encounter or use. We will explore a microcomputer-sized expert system in Chapter 3.

Our purpose here is to learn the basic principles of expert systems, and in these systems the inner workings are laid bare for our study. If you want to bake a cake, buy a mix or follow a recipe. But if you want to understand baking, watch the chefs who first work out the recipes and who do everything from scratch. The builders of these four expert systems had no recipes to follow, so these systems took years of trial and error to develop. Their pioneering work makes it possible for you and me to purchase programs off the shelf to help us develop our own expert system to run on our personal computers.

First we will re-introduce you to Prospector and Mycin, which you met in Chapter 1.

Prospector

Prospector's name describes its task. It helps geologists find likely sites to mine for scarce minerals. Even though it resides in a computer at SRI International, a research institute near San Francisco, it can help identify commercially valuable ore deposits anywhere in the world. It was developed at Stanford Research Institute in the late 1970s by Rene Reboh, the United States Geological Survey geologist Dennis Cox, and others. It identified its first commercially valuable ore deposit in 1981—a molybdenum deposit in eastern Washington state valued at up to $100,000,000.

How Prospector Is Used

Geologists scout many likely areas. They know in general what kinds of areas are favorable for different kinds of ores, but these areas might be acres or square miles in size. But what is the likelihood of finding commercial quantities of the ore in an area, and exactly where in the area should they dig? The geologists take detailed observations of the rock types and formations, and bring these back to Prospector.

The geologist sits down at the computer containing the Prospector program, and enters the pertinent data from the field observations.

```
Geol: There is quartz monzonite
Prosp: Quartz monzonite(5)    [Prospector responds]
G: There is cretaceous dike
P: Cretaceous dike(5)
G: There is sericite and pyrite
P: Sericite(5) pyrite(5)
G: There may be biotite
P: Biotite(2)
```

The numbers in parentheses are the degree of certainty assigned to each observation. "5" means "it is definitely there" and "–5" means "it is definitely not there." "0" means "I don't know." Prospector assigns these levels based on the geologist's statements. "There is pyrite" rates a 5, while "there may be biotite" rates a 2. A "probably isn't" statement would rate a –2.

Next the geologist and Prospector engage in a "consultative dialogue." Prospector flashes questions on the screen and the geologist answers them:

```
Pros: I am considering the possibility of
a Type-A porphyry copper deposit in the
target area.
The following questions are intended to
establish the nature of the petrotectonic
setting.

1. To what degree do you believe that the
target area is in a continental margin
mobile belt?

Geo: -2
```

This negative response suggests that Prospector should try a different line of inquiry. It's not important that you understand the technical terms in this dialogue. You should see that jargon terms like "granitic intrusives" and "petrotectonic" are "natural language" to geologists. So Prospector converses with geologists in the same language they use with one another, rather than in numbers and terse symbols. This is a key feature of many expert systems.

```
Pros: The following questions are intended
to determine the nature of the regional
environment.
2. To what degree do you believe that
there are granitic intrusives in the
region?

Geo: 5            [He's certain they are there.]

3. To what degree do you believe that the
region contains an abundance of small
stocks?
```

```
Geo: -3        [He's pretty sure they aren't there.]
```

As so on until,

```
Pros: To what degree do you believe that
igneous rocks in the region have
porphyritic texture?

Geo: Why?

Pros: I am trying to establish whether
some of the intrusive rocks in your area
have textures suggestive of a hypabyssal
to subvolcanic environment...
```

Like many expert systems, Prospector can "explain" its requests and its conclusions. This is a "canned" response, stored in Prospector especially to respond to "Why?" queries at this point. Prospector then repeats question #8, and the geologist responds with a "5" of certainty. Then Prospector concludes:

```
Pros: My certainty in hypabyssal nature
of the regional environment is now 4.924.
```

Questioning continues to narrow down the specific area and the particular ores to be found there. Prospector finally reaches a conclusion that looks like this:

```
On a scale from -5 to 5, my certainty
that there are alteration zones that are
favorable for a Type-A porphyry copper
deposit is now 4.833.
```

Notice that it doesn't answer "Yes, the ore is there," or "No, it's not there," but offers a confidence level that a commercial quantity of ore is there. Prospector states the factors upon which this conclusion is based:

```
There are two favorable factors; in order
of importance:
There is a sericitic zone in Zone 1 (4.834)
There is a potassic zone in Zone 2 (4.499)
```

Then Prospector finishes up by stating:

```
There are many factors that would have
been unfavorable had no favorable factor
existed to override them; in order of
importance:
There is a barren core zone in Zone 1
(-5.0)
There is a propylitic zone in Zone 2
(-4.989)
```

Prospector's Expertise

How does Prospector do this? It contains models of the terrain favorable to finding several different types of minerals. As the geologists feed in data from their observations, Prospector matches these statements with its internal model. As you saw, whenever it lacks info needed to reach a conclusion, it requests more by asking questions.

These models were built up over time by extensive interviews with many expert geologists, and boiling down the essence of how they identify favorable sites for mining or drilling. In Chapter 4, we will show you this process of extracting the needed knowledge from the experts and putting it into expert systems.

Prospector's Value

Prospector is like a team of experts representing many fields of geology who have all the facts at hand and are always available to pore over reams of data from varied sources. But the experts who initially contributed their knowledge from which its models were built certainly could not be kept together.

A valuable use for Prospector and other related expert systems is to sift quite rapidly through initial observational data on a large number of sites, and eliminate the vast majority of them. It would then point its users to the small proportion of likely sites on which they should focus their attention.

The knowledge to interpret the observations for each type of mineral is kept in a separate "knowledge base." Up to now, Prospector contains knowledge bases for finding about a dozen different kinds of deposits. Prospector, in common with virtually every expert system, has a very important feature: Its knowledge base about a particular mineral can be stripped out, leaving intact Prospector's general framework for reaching conclusions, and a knowledge base for another type of mineral can be built in.

So Prospector could be adapted to find likely locations to drill for oil or natural gas, or to find minerals on the ocean floor. Experts would first have to develop the extensive knowledge bases and models needed to identify these other resources. But once done, Prospector and its descendants could be programmed to sift through warehouses of data gathered from such sources as Landsat resource scanning satellites to identify scarce resources at much less cost than having trained geologists sift through the same data.

People often express concern that computers will take over all the tasks and leave nothing for us. Do the geologists resent having such a tool take over part of their jobs? Dennis Cox, a USGS geologist who helped build Prospector's knowledge base, says he will be happy if Prospector relieves him from having to sit in Alaska in the rain making elementary assessments. He would get more time to engage in productive research, and be able to disseminate his knowledge to many more people.

So the value of Prospector is similar to that of many other computer programs: It handles the drudgework, remembers all the tiny details, and frees up the humans for the more interesting tasks.

Mycin Diagnoses Infectious Blood Diseases

Each year two million people get sick while in hospitals recovering from something else, and perhaps 50,000 of them die. The cause is hospital-borne infections, introduced oftentimes by doctors and nurses themselves. These are often called "secondary infections," and they may develop unnoticed while the doctor focuses on the primary problem. Other thousands die or have strong reactions to the antibiotics they receive.

In Chapter 1 we introduced you to Mycin. You saw the doctor work with Mycin to diagnose hospital-born meningitis, and then select

"Prospector"

the best combination of antibiotics. We mentioned several features of Mycin, and now we will elaborate a bit on some of them.

We can learn a lot about expert systems by seeing how Mycin does its job, so we will come back to it throughout this book. Mycin is like the Model A Ford of expert systems. It is much easier to learn about cars by looking under the hood of a Model A than a Ferrari. Much more of Mycin is accessible compared to the slickly packaged programs now emerging. It's all there in plain view for us to study and learn from. Many of the basic features of expert systems were worked out by Mycin's developers. Several successful expert systems are direct descendants of Mycin, and all systems have benefitted from Mycin's lessons.

Mycin's Knowledge

In Chapter 1, you saw the doctor interact with Mycin in a "consultative dialogue" to discover the unexpected meningitis and to select the best drug treatment. How does Mycin do this? The Mycin software program contains the knowledge of many expert medical diagnosticians, built into the program as rules which look like these:

> *If*   1) the gram stain of the organism is gram negative, and
>   2) the morphology of the organism is rod, and
>   3) the aerobicity of the organism is anaerobic,
> *Then*   there is suggestive evidence (.7) that the identity of the organism is bacteroides.

This rule connects the result of the gram stain lab test to a particular microbe. Notice the decimal number (.7) in Mycin's diagnostic rule. This is called a certainty factor, which is an informal measure of the likelihood that the rule will be true in a particular case. It is like your weather forecaster saying, "There is a 70 percent chance it will rain tomorrow."

In medical diagnosis, what you don't find is as important as what you do find. Here is a rule which allows Mycin to take into consideration some negative findings:

> *If*   the identity of the organism is not known, and the gram stain of the organism is not known, and the morphology of the organism is not known, and the site of the culture is csf, and the infection is meningitis, and the age of the patient is 17 or less,
> *Then*   (.3) the category of the organism is enterobacteriaceae

This ".3" means that, given what little is known, it is unsafe to conclude that the organism is enterobacteriaceae.

Mycin has a separate set of rules for diagnosing the disease and for prescribing the antibiotics, about 500 in all, which cover dozens of disease conditions. Here is one of the rules used in the prescribing phase, which warns not to use tetracycline for young children.

If   1) the therapy under consideration is tetracycline, and

2) the age of the patient is less than 13

Then   there is strongly suggestive evidence (.8) that tetracycline is not a potential therapy for use against the organism.

The doctor using Mycin may never see these rules during normal operation. But while the doctor is feeding info into Mycin on a particular patient's case, Mycin searches through all these rules to find the ones which match up best with this data. We'll show you in Chapter 5 how Mycin searches through its rules.

Solid Conclusions in the Face of Uncertainty

One thing experts do well is to make good decisions before all the facts are available. Doctors making diagnoses must do this every day. Mycin would be useless unless it had this capability. Yet this is something which most software programs just cannot do.

Often, Mycin cannot reach a conclusion in a single step. Even after requesting additional data from its users, it finds links among several related rules, and works back through several rules until either its first hypothesis is shown to be incorrect, or until it is supported by the observed evidence. This process of working backwards through the rules is called "backward chaining" and will be explored more thoroughly in Chapter 5.

Even so, Mycin's conclusions are not certain. Mycin has a way of calculating with its certainty factors and confidence levels which allows it to combine several sources of uncertain evidence to reach conclusions with a high level of confidence and reliability. This is an essential ability for many expert systems.

It lists, not just the conclusion with the highest certainty factor, but several conclusions that are consistent with the evidence, and ranks them by their certainty factors. In Mycin, this feature is crucial for two reasons: First, since the conclusion is uncertain, obviously the doctor will want to check the other strong possibilities. But equally important, the patient may well have more than one infection that must be treated.

Mycin can give reasons for its decisions by retracing the ones it has invoked to reach its conclusion, and recapping them to the user in "canned" statements in natural English. In Chapter 1, we saw an example of this when the doctor asked why Mycin had asked a particular question. Here is another example that would arise when Mycin is prescribing antibiotics. Doctor:

```
Why did you give chloramphenicol for
E.coli in recommendation 1?
```

Mycin:

```
Chloramphenicol was prescribed for Item 2
in recommendation 1
   Since
   Chloramphenicol is a treatment of
choice for E.coli in meningitis.
   Item 2 is sensitive to Chloramphenicol.
   There were no contraindications for it.
Chloramphenicol was prescribed because it
was part of the recommendation that covers
for all of the items, using the fewest
number of drugs.
```

This is essential for Mycin. Since its conclusions are reached with only a certain level of certainty, this means that sometimes they will be incorrect. Since the doctors using Mycin are often facing life-or-death decisions, they want to doublecheck its reasoning very closely. When errors are found, the doctors can trace its reasoning back step-by-step and find the source—usually an inadequacy in one of the knowledge rules Mycin contains. Mycin is constructed so that the individual rules can be easily refined, added to, or deleted without disrupting the entire set of rules. In this way, its users can continually hone its performance based on their experience with it.

Why Mycin Is Needed

Mycin and related expert systems for medical diagnoses provide a much needed check. Very few physicians go through such a methodical decision process. As a result, they are often uncertain of what secondary infections may be present, so to cover all the bases, they sometimes have overprescribed antibiotics beyond what is required or even safe. The results of this practice can be worse than the disease being treated.

Mycin reaches reliable conclusions in a very high proportion of cases, even though it bases its reasoning on incomplete, uncertain, and even conflicting input. This is exactly why an expert system is needed. If a given symptom pointed reliably to a particular infection, if the doctor had all the time to get complete test results, and if the effects of each drug on each patient were known, then an expert system would be unnecessary.

R1 CONFIGURES LARGE COMPUTER SYSTEMS

If you have bought a personal computer recently, say an Apple Macintosh, you know you can buy a complete off-the-shelf package. The screen and keyboard are built in, and the other things you want, like a printer or extra disk drives, can just be plugged into the marked slots, and you are ready to compute.

With larger computers it is not so simple. DEC (Digital Equipment Corp.) makes VAX minicomputers, which are very popular in businesses and colleges. (Minicomputers are between microcomputers and mainframe computers in size and price.) When a company buys a VAX system, it buys a lot of specialized components, depending on its needs. Whenever a customer places an order, DEC must check to ensure that all the components ordered can fit together and operate together. These are very large and complex custom installations with components built into cabinet units and connected by cables which will run throughout an office or building. DEC used to rely solely on its technicians and sales representatives to check these orders. But as DEC grew, and VAX systems got larger and more complex, this task of configuring the computer systems got to be too much for the technicians.

So DEC developed an expert system, R1, to configure, or design the layout of, its VAX computers and peripherals. (R1 is also called XCON, for "eXpert CONfigurer.") R1 was developed initially at Carnegie-Mellon University in Pittsburgh in 1979, then brought into

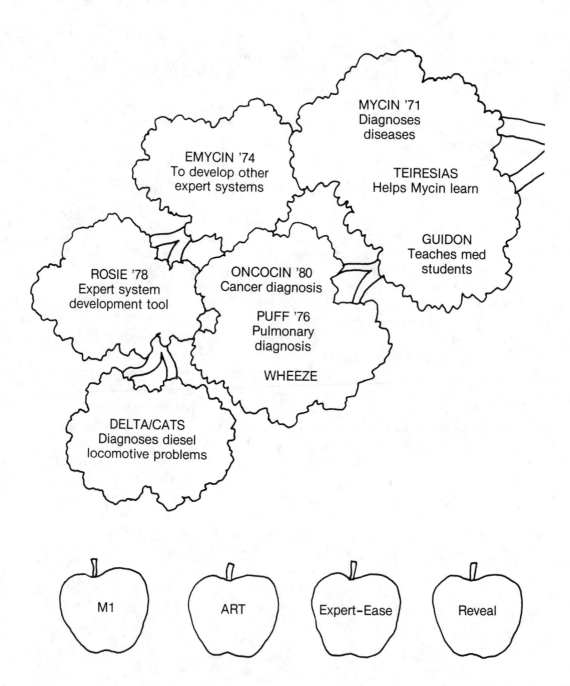

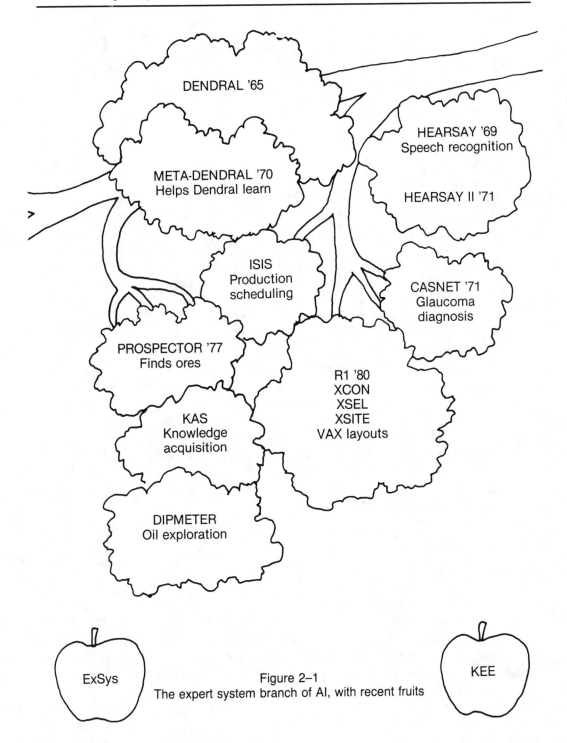

Figure 2–1
The expert system branch of AI, with recent fruits

successful commercial use by DEC over the next several years. By the early 1980s, DEC was relying heavily on R1 to configure ever larger and more complex computer systems. By now, it has far exceeded the abilities of the people who used to configure the systems.

R1 in the Field

Here's how R1 works. A DEC salesperson, who is a highly-trained computer technician, sits in the customer's office. She carries a small portable computer, plugs it into a phone line, and connects directly to the VAX computer in DEC's main office which contains R1. The technician types in all the information about the customer's desired system, for example, what type of central VAX computer is being ordered, what special modules it must have built into cabinets, where all the remote terminals and printers and mass storage units will go. She even types in information about the building. Will the air conditioning maintain a steady, cool temperature? Are the doors wide enough to get the computers through?

After all this data is typed in, R1 goes to work to design the best layout. First, it reviews the customer's order to spot any major discrepancies, such as essential components missing, incompatible items, etc. Next, it arranges the appropriate components in the central computer cabinet and the other cabinets. Then it designs the layout of the whole system on a floor plan of the customer's building, and finally designs the layout of the cabling between all the components. If R1 finds a problem with the design, it states what is wrong, tells how to correct the problem, then produces a detailed layout plan.

R1's Knowledge

R1 contains different knowledge rules and procedures for each step. As we will relate in detail in Chapter 4, these rules were built up over several years, and were based on the hands-on experience of numerous people responsible for configuring the computers. It currently has over 3300 rules and 2000 component descriptions. Here's just one rule:

> *If* the current subtask is assigning devices to unibus modules and there is an unassigned dual port disk drive and the type of controller it requires is known and there are two such controllers, neither of which has any devices assigned to it and the number of devices which these controllers can support is known
>
> *Then* assign the disk drive to each controller and note that each controller supports one device

R1, unlike Mycin and Prospector, doesn't carry on a dialogue with the technician as it is designing. After she puts in all the information needed, R1 chugs away until the configuration is completed. For a typical layout, R1 will go through 1000 rules and 250 product descriptions. This takes only about two minutes.

DEC Relies on R1

R1's value lies in its reliability, and in its ability to hold in memory the large number of configuration rules and components required. There are many ways to configure a particular system, but R1 comes up with an efficient and optimal configuration virtually every time. Its results are checked by its operators, and are consistently as good or better than the best they could do. After several years of everyday use, during which time DEC has steadily developed larger and more complex computer systems, and increased its volume of business, it would be virtually impossible to return R1's task to human order checkers.

Dendral Predicts Molecular Structures of Unknown Compounds

Impurities in the metal of an aircraft fuselage lead to metal fatigue and cause a crash. What is the impurity? A wildlife refuge is threatened by minute amounts of a pesticide from agricultural irrigation runoff which drains into the refuge. Exactly what substance is sickening the fish and birds, and what is its source? Students in a brand-new school are getting sick. It must be caused by some toxic gas exuded by the new building materials. But what is it, and how is it making the kids sick?

Chemists must identify the chemical structure of the unknown compound causing the problem before they can know where it comes from and what to do about it. The normal method for identifying the substance is called "mass spectrometry." A small sample of the compound is bombarded with high-energy radiation. The radiation is broken apart by the compound the way a prism breaks apart sunlight into a band of colors. Each compound will scatter the radiation in a slightly different pattern, depending on its atomic makeup, and the way the atoms are arranged. This is called a "mass spectogram" and Figure 2-2 shows one example.

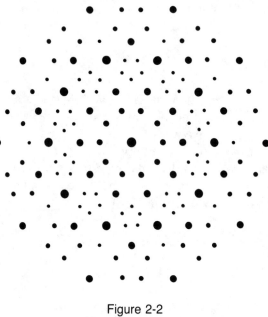

Figure 2-2
Mass Spectogram

This is a bit like trying to deduce the nature of an object by watching its shadows dance on the wall. Chemists have learned through the years what patterns are made by many common groups of atoms. But there are literally millions of possibilities. And in crisis situations, there is no time to sift through them all.

An expert system called Dendral was developed to greatly speed up the process of identifying the structure of these unknown compounds. Dendral is really the grand-daddy of expert systems. It was born at Stanford University in 1965, by Nobel Prize winner Joshua Lederburg and Edward Feigenbaum, a leader in expert systems research. After several years of development and testing, Dendral became operational in the early 1970s. This shows you how long the oldest expert systems have been around, and how long it took to develop them. It is now in daily use by chemists all over the country. For some of its tasks, Dendral is better than any human expert, and it has redefined the division of labor between man and machine in its field.

How Dendral Is Used

Suppose we have a blood sample from one of these sick kids. First the chemist in his lab separates everything out of the sample that he knows isn't causing the problem. He isolates a minute sample of one or more unknown chemicals. This sample is subjected to the mass spectrometry process we described, producing a pattern like the one above. Then the chemist carefully records the pattern in a graph and turns the job over to Dendral.

First, Dendral reduces the millions of possible structures down to a handful. By examining the pattern reported to it by the chemist, it deduces what molecular fragments must be present, and what fragments cannot be present. It knows this because each fragment produces a unique set of peaks on its graph.

So Dendral reasons like this: The unknown substance must have molecular fragments A and B, and it cannot have fragments C or D. So Dendral goes through its list of all the possibilities, and eliminates all these with either C or D. Then it eliminates all those which lack either A or B. This leaves just a few possibilities. Dendral lists these remaining candidates. Second, Dendral tests each of these remaining possibilities by comparing what kind of spectrogram pattern it should have, to the actual pattern of the compound the chemist is studying.

Have Dendral, Will Travel

Dendral doesn't engage in dialogue with the chemist like Mycin or Prospector do. The chemist enters the initial data, then Dendral chomps through all its knowledge of chemical structure until it produces the solution. This has been called the "hired gun" model of interaction.

Dendral's Knowledge

Dendral contains not one, but two types of expertise, one type for each of these two stages. In its first stage, it has many rules derived from the experience of many chemists in matching spectrogram patterns with chemical constituents. These allow Dendral to prune the search down to a manageable number, but seldom down to just one possibility.

In the second stage, Dendral has a set of rules which allow it to calculate all possible molecular structures which have a particular combination of atoms. Even Dendral must prune down the number of possible structures it considers in Stage 2. In principle, it could evaluate every possible combination, but this would be too much for even the largest computer.

Why Dendral Is Interesting

Dendral performs a pretty abstruse task, even though an important one. We described it here for a couple of reasons besides respect for its venerable position as patriarch of the expert system clan. The expert systems we have described in this chapter represent the four most successful approaches to building expert systems so far. Dendral is the best example of the "generate and test" variety. That is, it works by first generating a list of possible structures, and then testing each one against a model, to see which best fits the facts of the case. Secondly, Dendral's task can be compared to the wind tunnel simulator we are going to describe next, which is not an expert system. Contrasting the two will help us understand the difference.

Aircraft Design—Complex Program but Not an Expert System

Both NASA and major aircraft manufacturers use supercomputers to simulate the action of wind tunnels to help design advanced aircraft bodies. For each design, they must know what parts of the body provide lift, what parts cause drag and friction, where the air moves in smooth sheets along the body, and where it becomes turbulent. They have huge wind tunnels, build meticulous scale models of proposed aircraft, conduct repeated tests of their flight characteristics in the wind tunnel, and take painstaking measurements.

But they no longer rely on the physical wind tunnel. They can use a supercomputer to simulate the action of a particular airframe in the wind tunnel. It all takes place within the computer. They are able to do this using a branch of mathematics called "computational fluid dynamics." Since air is a fluid, this mouthful simply means using a computer to study how air flows around a body.

This sounds about as arcane and complex as Dendral's job of predicting structures of complex molecules, doesn't it? But there is a major difference. The knowledge which goes into fluid dynamics has been totally reduced to mathematical formulas. Even the shapes of the aircraft are entirely described using math formulas. Most of the formulas are of incredible complexity, yet nevertheless they are completely reduced to numbers.

The significance of that to us is that for any particular simulation, a set of numbers can be plugged into these formulas, and the supercomputer will reach a single definite solution. Just like $1 + 1 = 2$. Same answer every time. Dendral's knowledge, like that of every other expert system, cannot be reduced completely to numbers. The scientists just don't know enough about the subject to state a complete, all-inclusive theory which covers every possibility. So it is not the complexity of the task, per se, which calls for an expert system, rather the type of knowledge required to solve the problem.

COMMON CHARACTERISTICS OF EXPERT SYSTEM TASKS

There are many possible solutions. It would take too long to examine each one.

The problem-solving expertise is conceptual; can't be reduced to numbers.

The information needed is incomplete, uncertain, subjective, inconsistent, subject to change. The program can work with incomplete data.

The conclusions reached will often be uncertain. The expert system will state that it has only a certain level of confidence that its answer is correct. It will rank conclusions by their likelihood of being correct.

Experts may disagree on how to solve the problem.

The task is always changing and evolving.

The cost of a poor or late decision is very high.

COMMON CHARACTERISTICS OF EXPERT SYSTEM TASKS

You have seen four different expert systems—Prospector, Mycin, R1, and Dendral—which handle four very different tasks. You just got a glimpse of a computer program which does not use an expert system, even though its task is equally complex. As varied as these expert systems are, there are important commonalities in the situations they deal with. These dictate the design of the expert systems, and set them apart from conventional software. Let's pull together these common features, and contrast them with a piece of conventional software, like our airframe tester, or an accounting program.

CONTRASTING CHARACTERISTICS OF CONVENTIONAL SOFTWARE

All the decision rules in the program and all the data fed in to solve the problem must be reduced to numbers and formulas.

For any set of data, there is only one solution.

If any data is missing, the computer cannot reach a solution.

The solution will be stated with no uncertainty. Even if a solution is stated as a probability, the computer is certain that it is the one and only probability that fits the data.

There is a generally accepted way to solve the problem.

The task changes relatively little over time.

Many Possible Solutions

The first thing you notice is that each expert system had a very large number of possible alternatives that had to be examined. It would take far too long to examine and evaluate each one separately. In fact, it may be impossible. In AI jargon, the "problem space" is very large and uncertain. You saw that with Dendral's task, there are millions of possible molecular structures. In Mycin, the factors are so numerous that a doctor can easily neglect a critical one. Prospector is examining the whole outdoors, and R1 has a virtually unlimited number of possible design variations.

Conclusions Are Not Certain

Expert systems often cannot give straight yes or no answers. You saw that Prospector and Mycin's conclusions were stated with a degree of likelihood which can't be accurately known. As a result, as with a human expert, some of their conclusions will be wrong, even when based on good rules. Many of their knowledge rules are designed to limit this uncertainty to manageable levels. They are both programmed to request additional data until they have enough, and to explain their behavior. We'll see how they do this in Chapter 5.

As a matter of fact, with expert systems, there may be no single best solution. Several problems may be intermixed. A patient being considered by Mycin may have more than one disease, any of which could be deadly. When prescribing drugs, the best drug available may cause allergic reactions in the patient. A trade-off is necessary. With Dendral, the substance being examined may be a mixture of more than one compound, and Dendral is expected to identify them all.

Contrast all this with an accounting task. For any set of numbers, there is just one right answer. When you put all your financial data into the income statement, there is only one correct figure for the bottom line. Likewise with our wind tunnel simulator. For any set of values plugged into it, the formulas will return just one solution.

Fuzzy Data

Expert systems reach uncertain conclusions because the information that they use is often incomplete, uncertain, subjective, inconsistent, subject to change, and even plain old wrong. And just like any high-priced consultant, the expert systems are expected to give good, reliable advice anyway.

Medicine, geology and computer system configuration are not exact sciences. Doctors and geologists assign certainty factors on an intuitive basis. Let's look at just some of the sources of uncertainty in medical diagnosis. The symptoms observed by the doctor may signify any of several illnesses. How many illnesses cause dizziness and vomiting, for example? Lab tests, even if they are available, are not certain. Next consider the problem of prescribing drugs. Each patient has different drug tolerances and sensitivities, which can only be known approximately. Drugs are always changing. New ones come out, and research turns up new facts about them. Even diseases change: A strain of microbes becomes resistant to drugs that previously knocked it cold. In contrast, the data that goes into a financial statement must be complete and internally consistent. Discrepancies can be pursued down to the penny.

The Knowledge Is Conceptual, Not Numerical

To make it even more of a challenge for our expert systems, the facts and knowledge they use is mostly in the form of concepts. It is impossible to reduce these rules to numbers, which conventional software requires.

The Experts Often Disagree

They do things in different ways, and more than one way works. There are no solid theories linking observations or evidence to particular conclusions, but just experts' rules of thumb built up through years of experience. If patients recover, if ores are found, the rules must have been pretty good. These rules get sharpened through use.

Many tackle complex social or physical problems that just cannot be described completely. Consider Mycin, linking observed symptoms to particular microbes; or Prospector, linking surface rocks to commercial ore concentrations. With Dendral, chemists were so far from being able to describe the constraints from mass spectrograms fully that it was worth the effort to develop Meta-Dendral to help develop these rules.

No single person has all the knowledge required to tackle any of these tasks. The people who develop expert systems must figure out how knowledge from diverse specialties and disagreeing experts can be integrated into one system. But every accountant proceeds according to generally accepted accounting principles. And the wind tunnel simulator is based on a complete theory and a comprehensive set of mathematical formulas.

Things Are Always Changing

The tasks for which expert systems are needed are ones in which constant change is taking place. What was adequate last year is outmoded next year. New knowledge and requirements constantly emerge. With R1, for example, as soon as it mastered one VAX system, DEC expanded it to handle ever larger ones, and then sold more of them.

WHAT TASKS ARE EXPERT SYSTEMS RIGHT FOR?

TOO EASY *"Use Conventional Software"*	JUST RIGHT	TOO HARD *"Requires Human Intelligence"*
Payroll, Inventory	Diagnosing & troubleshooting	Designing new tools
Tax returns	Analyzing diverse data	Stock market prediction
Orbits and trajectories	Production scheduling	Discovering new principles
Database management	Equipment layout	Everyday language "Common sense" problems
Facts are known precisely, exactly; they are reduced to numbers.	Facts are known but not precisely; they are stated as ideas.	Requires innovation or discovery, or "common sense."
Expertise is cheap.	Expertise is expensive but available.	Expertise is not available or nobody knows enough to be an expert.

With Mycin, drugs are always changing, but even the microbes mutate so they resist formerly potent drugs.

If the tasks weren't continually changing, many of these expert systems probably wouldn't be needed. The experts would soon define all the relationships, and they could then be reduced to exact formulas, as is the case with the fluid dynamics theory the wind tunnel simulator uses.

Important Decisions

The decisions for which expert systems are used are important enough that they must be made quickly and accurately even in the face of all these hurdles, and will justify the high cost of developing such systems. Of course this is also true for any conventional software program. But as we will see in Chapter 4, expert systems have been exceptionally expensive and time-consuming to develop.

Now it is time to leave the mainframe computer expert systems for a while. In the next chapter, we will roll our sleeves up and try our hand at putting together a simple expert system, using Expert-Ease, a software package that runs on an IBM PC. By trying it ourselves, we will learn a lot more about what is involved.

BENEFITS OF EXPERT SYSTEMS COMPARED TO HUMAN EXPERTS

Best expertise in the field is made available to many more people. Tough problems can be solved even when expert is not present.

Very thorough and systematic; no factors forgotten. Easy to keep adding in new knowledge as it is available.

Allows experts to handle even more complex problems rapidly and reliably.

Top experts' knowledge gets saved, rather than being lost, when they retire.

Used as learning tool. Many more can learn what the masters know.

Helps clarify the knowledge and effective problem-solving approaches in the field.

Can integrate knowledge from several fields.

CHAPTER 3

DEVELOPING
A SMALL-SCALE
EXPERT SYSTEM

- **A Couple of "Real" Examples to Demonstrate Basic
  Principles of Building an Expert System**
- **Good and Bad Tasks for Expert Systems**
- **Building Up Your Expertise from Examples**
- **Your System Improves With Use**

What better way to learn about expert systems than to pretend we are building our own? We will walk through a couple of very simplified expert systems to demonstrate some of the principles that guide the development and use of any expert system, no matter how large and sophisticated. We will discover what kinds of tasks you should and shouldn't use an expert system for. We will see how to build up expertise by putting in examples of the kinds of things we want the expert system to do. Once we get a prototype expert system built, we will see how it performs and how to improve it through use. To help us develop our system, we will use Expert-Ease, a software program designed to help people build their own expert system. Expert-Ease and the expert systems we will design run on a personal computer such as the IBM PC.

CHOOSING THE TASK FOR OUR EXPERT SYSTEM

Building a useful expert system takes much time and effort. So unless we are building one for the love of tinkering on the computer, it should be for some purpose that is very important to us. Well now, what's a good reason to build an expert system? Let's build an expert system to get rich quick. What better way of getting rich than playing the stock market? Suppose we build an expert system to predict stock prices. Before we start spending our fortune, however, we need to find out whether predicting the stock market is an appropriate task for an expert system. Expert-Ease points the way.

The Stock Price Predictor

Let's put the Expert-Ease disk into our computer and get to work. Built into Expert-Ease is a program to help us decide whether we should attempt to build an expert system for a particular task based on our answers to four questions that it will flash on the computer screen. So let's test our idea for predicting stock prices. The first question:

```
Are the answers to your problem or your
decisions determined at random?

1. Yes
2. No
```

We enter "no," because even stock prices don't move at random. It is impossible to build an expert system for any problem with random or unpredictable solutions.

```
How important is accuracy in the answers
or decisions? What is the consequence of
a wrong answer or decision?

1. I need total accuracy. The consequences
of a wrong answer or decision are
catastrophic.
```

```
2. Accuracy is important. I can tolerate
occasional wrong answers, but I need the
right answers most of the time.

3. While accuracy is still important, I
can tolerate initial errors as long as I
can adapt the system to new or changing
circumstances?
```

We select #2. A handful of bad recommendations could clean us out.
A wealthier investor might select #3.

```
How complete is the set of examples
describing your problem or decision?

1. My set of examples is 100% complete,
and covers every possible case which
could arise.

2. My set of examples is almost complete.
I think it covers most cases which will
arise.

3. My set of examples covers only a small
number of the possible situations which
could occur.

4. My set of examples covers a fair number
of the possible situations which could
occur.
```

We select #3 here.

```
How well will the people who will use the
system be able to detect wrong answers?

1. The people who will use the system are
capable of spotting wrong answers. They
can compensate for flaws or gaps in the
set of examples.

2. The people who will use the system will
not be able to detect wrong answers.
```

We select #1 for this one. We will be very aware of wrong stock
selections. As soon as we enter our answer to this last question,
Expert-Ease comes back with its recommendation:

```
We would advise you not to use Expert-Ease
for this problem. You will get an
unacceptable level of wrong answers
because your examples do not cover enough
situations.
```

What a disappointment! Expert-Ease recommends we don't try building a system to predict stock prices because we don't know enough about the field and the cost of a bad decision would be too high. So for a first principle, we must state the obvious:

> *Principle:* An expert system requires some real expertise in the field. Either you must be the expert, or be able to build the expertise through experience.

So if we are going to build an expert system to predict stock prices, we will have to find an expert who can help us. To find the best experts, suppose we research the various investment advisory bulletins. We would quickly discover two things:

1. The experts don't agree. Everyone has his or her own formula for winning in the stock market. There seems to be no way to reconcile the different approaches.

2. No one seems to have a surefire formula. Many people seem to be getting rich now, but many others who publicized winning formulas a few years ago are very quiet these days.

But suppose we find a very successful and experienced investor who is willing to share his or her expertise with us. Could we use that knowledge to build a useful expert system that would help us make better investment decisions? Perhaps we could. Throughout this book we will discuss a number of expert systems that help experts make better decisions. There is one thing to keep in mind, however: An expert system cannot perform any better than the experts do. How good is even an expert investor at accurately predicting the movement of any particular stock or stock market trend?

> *Principle:* Expert systems rarely perform better than the experts. The problems on which expert systems outperform human experts are not tasks about which they know more than the humans, but about which they forget less.

As we saw in Chapter 2, R1 designs computer layouts better than human technicians because it can hold more factors in its "mind" at once than can humans, and Dendral has a better record of identifying unknown chemical compounds than human experts do because it can consider more possible solutions more rapidly. Both of these are tasks, however, that humans *can* do well. No one has mastered tasks such as stock market prediction. There are too many reasons why a stock price can rise or fall and these depend on factors as varied as world politics, competitors' strategies, and the weather. Not only are these factors not understood well enough to be explained, but many are inherently unpredictable. And that makes a poor candidate for an expert system.

There are computer programs that predict stock market movement, although they are not expert systems. They are based on a lot of historical data that tracks the movements of technical stock market indicators. And the best of these are mere auxiliaries to human decision making. In this book, we will see not only the promise, but also the limitations of expert systems. This stock prediction example shows us some of the characteristics of a task that is too elusive to be tackled with an expert system. Now let's look at another kind of task.

WEATHER FORECASTING: A DOABLE TASK?

Since we aren't getting rich, let's at least stay comfortable. Let's see if we can create a system that will forecast the weather. We could continue to rely on the TV weather forecasters: Whatever they predict, prepare for the opposite. But since we probably think we are as much an expert as anyone, let's build our own.

Let's first see if this is a doable task. We'll again use the Expert-Ease task evaluator. But this time, instead of repeating all the choices, which are summarized in Figure 3–1, we'll just state our answer to each question.

```
Are the answers to your problem or your
decisions determined at random?

2. No

How important is accuracy in the answers
or decisions? What is the consequence of
a wrong answer or decision?
```

CHECKLIST FOR EXPERT SYSTEM TASKS
(from Expert-Ease task evaluator)

Are the answers to your problem or your decisions determined at random?

1. Yes
2. No

How important is accuracy in the answers or decisions? What is the consequence of a wrong answer or decision?

1. I need total accuracy. The consequences of a wrong answer or decision are catastrophic.
2. Accuracy is important. I can tolerate occasional wrong answers, but I need the right answers most of the time.
3. While accuracy is still important, I can tolerate initial errors as long as I can adapt the system to new or changing circumstances.

How complete is the set of examples describing your problem or decision?

1. My set of examples is 100% complete, and covers every possible case which could arise.
2. My set of examples is almost complete. I think it covers most cases which will arise.
3. My set of examples covers only a small number of the possible situations which could occur.
4. My set of examples covers a fair number of the possible situations which could occur.

How well will the people who will use the system be able to detect wrong answers?

1. The people who will use the system are capable of spotting wrong answers. They can compensate for flaws or gaps in the set of examples.
2. The people who will use the system will not be able to detect wrong answers.

```
3. While accuracy is still important, I
can tolerate initial errors as long as I
can adapt the system to new or changing
circumstances?

How complete is the set of examples
describing your problem or decision?

3. My set of examples covers only a small
number of the possible situations which
could occur.

How well will the people who will use the
system be able to detect wrong answers?

1. The people who will use the system are
capable of spotting wrong answers. They
can compensate for flaws or gaps in the
set of examples.
```

On the basis of these responses to its questions, Expert-Ease makes this recommendation:

```
We would advise you to use Expert-Ease.
You will get wrong answers initially, but
if you extend your examples as these new
situations occur, you will get your
desired level of accuracy.
```

Starting a New Expert System with Examples

How do we forecast the weather? Our basic premise for weather forecasting is that we can forecast what is most likely to happen tomorrow by observing what is happening today. Expert-Ease will help us build an expert system to forecast tomorrow's weather which is built on this premise. Expert-Ease allows us to build up our own expert system from examples. By putting in a number of instances of one day's weather related to the weather patterns of the preceding day, it can automatically develop rules that will forecast future weather. By building predictive rules from the examples we enter, Expert-Ease helps us create a working expert system, even though we are not expert meteorologists.

Even so, we still have to know something about the weather to come up with meaningful examples. To start with, we must have some idea of what the important predictive factors are. For example, we know that if—where we live—today it is cloudy, and the wind is from the southwest, we had better take our umbrella tomorrow.

Expert-Ease guides us in starting our system by asking what it is we want to predict, and what the key predictive factors are. We wish to forecast the next day's weather, so we first enter that into Expert-Ease as the desired outcome. Expert-Ease then asks us to enter the most important factor influencing this outcome, then the second most important factor, and so on. So to start with, we will presume that the most important factors in predicting tomorrow's weather are the wind direction, what the sky looks like, and whether the barometer is rising or falling. We enter this outcome and these three predictive factors into Expert-Ease:

Wind is from: Sky is: Barometric pressure is: Next day's weather is:

Finally, Expert-Ease has us enter the important values for each of these factors. Based on our experience, we choose the following possibilities for each of these factors:

Wind is from: calm, southwest, northwest, or east
Sky is: cloudy blue partly cloudy
Barometric pressure is: rising falling or steady

This is similar to setting up a database or a spreadsheet. After we have these categories established, we can begin entering examples of weather each day. So let's start by recording these observations over a period of time, and then note the outcome the next day.

Suppose we do this for two weeks, and make the observations shown here:

DATE	WIND IS FROM	SKY IS	BAROMETRIC PRESSURE	NEXT DAY'S WEATHER
1	southwest	cloudy	falling	rain
2	southwest	cloudy	steady	cloudy
3	southwest	cloudy	rising	shine
4	calm	partly	steady	shine
5	northwest	blue	steady	shine
6	southwest	blue	falling	rain
7	southwest	cloudy	rising	shine
8	east	blue	steady	shine
9	calm	blue	steady	shine
10	northwest	blue	falling	cloudy
11	southwest	cloudy	falling	rain
12	east	cloudy	rising	cloudy
13	east	cloudy	steady	shine
14	calm	blue	rising	shine

We enter these into our computer using the format we set up with Expert-Ease.

Expert systems builders call this process of building up predictive rules from many instances *instantiation*. This is an essential process even for builders of professional systems because, as we will see in Chapter 4, experts don't always know what they know, so they clarify what they know about the task by talking about how they reached decisions in particular instances.

> *Principle:* Whether or not you are an expert, you can build up the kind of knowledge base needed by an expert system by recording a large number of examples or instances of the set of observations and what actually happened.

Try Our New System

After two weeks of recording data, we may feel that our prototype expert system is ready to test. How do we know when we reach that point? When it seems like few or no new patterns are emerging as examples. Even when we begin testing our system, we will continue adding daily observations to test our growing system. Expert-Ease has a "black box" that will take all our examples, and automatically develop from them a predictive rule. Figure 3-1 shows what this rule looks like.

It can now apply this rule to the subsequent observations we enter to forecast the following day's weather conditions. So let's now let our system use what it knows to forecast tomorrow's weather, and compare its forecasts with what actually happens. Each day we will record the sky, the wind, and the barometric pressure, enter these into Expert-Ease, and have it forecast the next day's weather. Then the next day, we will see what really happens, and compare the two to see how well our prototype system forecasts. Let's do this for ten days as shown on page 66.

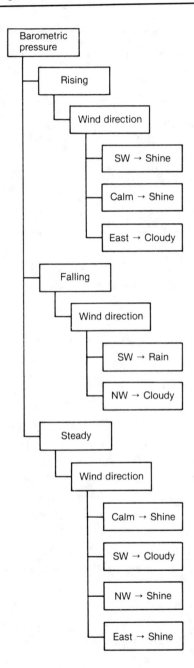

Figure 3–1
Initial decision rule

DATE	WIND IS FROM	SKY IS	BAROMETRIC PRESSURE	FORECAST WEATHER	ACTUAL WEATHER
15	southwest	cloudy	falling	rain	rain
16	southwest	cloudy	steady	cloudy	cloudy
17	southwest	cloudy	falling	*rain*	*shine*
18	southwest	cloudy	steady	*cloudy*	*rain*
19	southwest	cloudy	steady	*cloudy*	*rain*
20	calm	cloudy	steady	?	shine
21	southwest	blue	rising	*shine*	*rain*
22	northwest	cloudy	rising	?	rain
23	northwest	blue	rising	shine	shine
24	southwest	blue	falling	shine	shine

So, we see that our system made some good forecasts, and some poor ones. Just like the weather forecaster does.

Improving Your System's Performance

We want to improve the system's performance. To do so, let's go back to one of the days when the forecast went awry, and see if we can tell why. We see that on the 17th, our system predicted rain, and it was sunny. Why did our system not forecast accurately on the 17th? According to the rule Expert-Ease derived from our examples, it should have rained. Since it did not, there must be some other factors we did not take into consideration. Let's go back to our recorded observations of the 17th, and compare them to the observations of the 1st or the 11th, which were "well-behaved." We may be able to spot the discrepancies, find out what additional factors would account for them, and add them into our system to improve future forecasts.

Suppose that we discover that on the 17th, even though the barometer was falling, it was falling very slowly, and was still above 30.00. Upon reviewing all the other observations we recorded over the last couple of weeks, we see that whether the barometer is above or below 30.00 is important, and also see that wind speed is as important as wind direction. So let's add in more detail on barometric pressure and wind speed and see how this improves our predictions. We will go back to our Expert-Ease program, and add in two more factors:

Wind in knots:	10 knots or above, or below 10 knots
Barometric pressure:	30.00 or above, or below 30.00

We can then do what builders of larger expert systems do—test our refined system against forecasts with known outcomes. First we fill in the examples for the 1st through the 14th with these additional factors, and then have Expert-Ease produce a new decision rule for us, as shown in figure 3-2.

Next we will test this new rule against the data from the 15th through the 24th, to see how well it forecasts.

DATE	WIND IS FROM	WIND KNOTS	SKY IS	BAROMETER	PRESSURE	PREDICTED WEATHER	NEXT DAY'S
15	southwest	above 10	cloudy	29.90	falling	rain	rain
16	southwest	under 10	cloudy	30.05	steady	cloudy	cloudy
17	southwest	under 10	cloudy	30.05	falling	shine	shine
18	southwest	above 10	cloudy	29.85	steady	rain	rain
19	southwest	under 10	partly	30.05	steady	shine	rain
20	calm	under 10	cloudy	29.98	steady	shine	shine
21	southwest	above 10	blue	29.95	rising	rain	rain
22	northwest	above 10	cloudy	29.98	rising	rain	rain
23	northwest	under 10	blue	30.02	rising	shine	shine
24	southwest	under 10	blue	29.98	falling	shine	shine

That's quite an improvement in the accuracy of our system's forecasting. Even though it is still not 100 percent, adding these two factors has allowed us to make finer and more accurate forecasts.

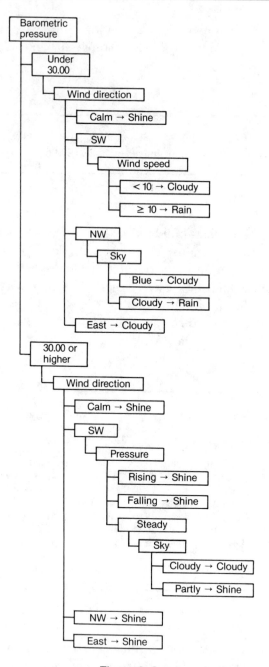

Figure 3–2
Refined decision rule

> *Principle:* The more accurate and pertinent and complete examples you put in, the better predictions it makes.

If we were recording all those observations from the first day, why didn't we program them into Expert-Ease from the beginning? We could have done so, but we wanted to illustrate a point. With large-scale expert systems, which have many more connections and rules programmed into them than we have here, it is very important to make the system as compact and efficient as possible. So expert system builders always strive for the smallest number of relationships which will allow them to have accurate forecasts.

This also illustrates another point. Even the top experts in a field cannot initially specify all the knowledge needed to build a useful and workable expert system. In Chapter 4, we will see that the process of building and refining an expert system has a large element of trial and error in it. We make our best guess about what knowledge is needed to make the system work, we test it, then we refine it and test it again.

> *Principle:* Building an expert system is a trial and error process.

As the ancient master says, "Every error is a learning opportunity." The expert system helps you in a very important way as you seek to improve its performance. Your expert system is excellent at pinpointing the source of its problems. You can improve its performance by refining it at the point at which it performs poorly. The days for which it makes poor forecasts point out the places where you need to make refinements. We did not have to go back and examine each day to find the cause for the poor forecast, just the 17th and the days which looked similar—the 1st and the 11th.

> *Principle:* The place where you find glitches in your program is the place to add more examples or to make corrections in your rules.

How Good Can the System Get?

We have tested our expert system, then refined and retested it, and it made better forecasts. Since the forecasts were still not 100 percent, we could go through another cycle of refining and retesting. As we keep entering data and refining our rules, we will find that our forecasts will get better and better. Since there are regularities in weather, over a period of time, we will be able to make some accurate forecasts about the weather tomorrow in our local area. Our system will be able to make forecasts such as, "There is a 30 percent chance of rain tomorrow."

Suppose we continue to develop and refine our system. Soon we have a few months' data, and we can make pretty good predictions. But then the season turns, the weather patterns change, and we must identify and enter a whole new set of relationships with new variables. We keep that up for a couple of years, and are again getting pretty good predictions year round. Then we have a particularly wet year. Then a couple of drought years. There is no end to the improvements we can make. But after a while we have so many factors to track that we discover they are taxing the capacity of our computer. And we still occasionally dress too warmly or leave our umbrella at home when it rains.

> *Principle:* The capacity of your computer often limits the capabilities of an expert system.

So what have we discovered? You need a certain number of instances or rules before you can use the system at all to make predictions. When it is first usable, its predictions are not very reliable. Additional instances and refinements quickly improve its reliability at first, as shown in Figure 3–3. But after some initial improvement, we would soon discover that it takes much more careful refinement to further improve its reliability significantly. The curve flattens out.

> *Principle:* The more examples you enter, the slower the rate of improvement for entering subsequent data.

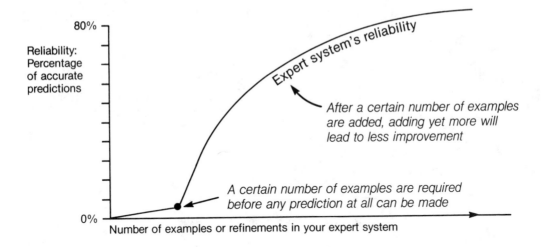

Figure 3–3
Improved performance with refinements

At Its Best, Is the System Worthwhile?

The key question now is, how good is our system's performance? Could it ever become good enough so that we would feel comfortable basing important decisions on its forecasts? Could it ever make predictions as well as we can just by glancing out our window? Yes, we probably could do substantially better than that. But we face two questions here:

1. Can the expert system be built? Is it feasible?
2. Is it worth the effort?

We are proud to say that our weather forecasting system has proven itself doable. For our local weather, we can make forecasts at least as well as the National Weather Service. Whether it is worth the effort is harder to answer. If it is better than an expert's performance, then the expert system may be worthwhile. But if its performance is still below the expert's, as shown in Figure 3–5, or even just a little better, then the expert system is probably not worth our while to build, except as an experiment or a hobby.

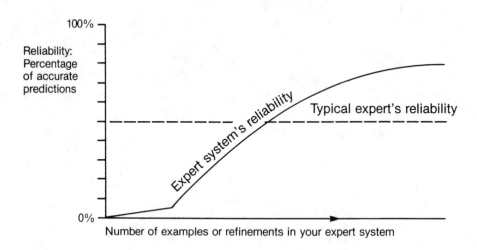

Figure 3–4
With refinement, system's performance surpasses expert's

These are exactly the issues that builders of large-scale expert systems face. Many expert systems development projects have foundered and gone under because the developers—or those footing the bill—came to realize that the potential benefits were just not going to justify the effort. This is a bit like having a home-computer program to balance your personal checkbook: It's easy to use, and perhaps faster and more accurate than we are, but for many people it just isn't worth the effort to use it.

How can we tell up front whether developing an expert system will be worthwhile? Throughout this book, we will look at several other expert systems which the developers feel have definitely paid for themselves, and in the last chapter we will summarize the reasons why.

Principle: An expert system must meet tests of feasibility and of being worth the effort.

Comparing the Weather and Stock Price Forecasters

Why did the weather forecasting system prove to be much more feasible than one for predicting the movement of stock prices? Although weather forecasting is a long way from being an exact science,

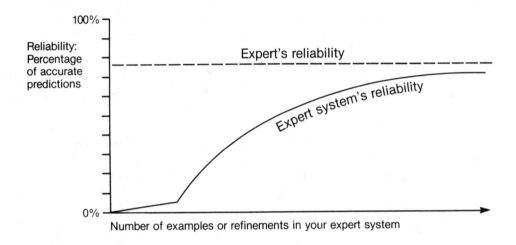

Figure 3–5
Even with refinement, performance falls short

there are discernible, repeating weather patterns. Even without understanding the underlying dynamics of the weather patterns we observed, we could identify a limited number of factors which had relatively consistent predictive value.

The movement of stock prices, on the other hand, is influenced by a much greater variety of factors—such things as the outcome of pending legislation, competitor's marketing strategies, changes in interest rates, economic and political developments in other parts of the world—even the weather. Many of these factors are inherently unpredictable, and even when we can predict them, we cannot accurately specify their impact on some stock price or market trend.

Now that we have glimpsed some of the nuts and bolts issues of creating a small expert system, let's look in more detail at the problem of getting the knowledge needed for a large-scale expert system into a computer.

PRINCIPLES FOR BUILDING EXPERT SYSTEMS

An expert system requires some real expertise in the field. Either you must be the expert, or be able to build the expertise through experience.

Expert systems rarely perform better than the experts. The problems on which expert systems outperform human experts are not tasks about which they know more than the humans, but about which they forget less.

Whether or not you are an expert, you can build up the kind of knowledge base needed by an expert system by recording a large number of examples or instances of the set of observations and what actually happened.

Building an expert system is a trial and error process.

The place where you find glitches in your program is the place to add more examples or to make corrections in your rules.

The more accurate and pertinent and complete examples you put in, the better predictions it makes.

After a certain point, the more examples you enter, the slower the rate of improvement for entering subsequent data.

The capacity of your computer often limits the capabilities of an expert system.

An expert system must meet tests of feasibility and of being worth the effort.

"9 to 5"

CHAPTER 4

GETTING KNOWLEDGE INTO THE COMPUTER

- **Knowledge acquisition—How an Expert System Learns or Acquires Its Knowledge**
- **The Knowledge Engineer and the Domain Expert**
- **The Knowledge Base and the Inference Engine**

In this chapter we return our attention to large-scale expert systems. Our basic question for this chapter is, "How does an expert's knowledge get into a computer, so that the computer can manipulate this knowledge to reach a desired conclusion?"

This is not an easy task. It is much more difficult than putting data into conventional software programs, or even programming them. Normally we can just hire people to enter data into a program, but entering "knowledge" is a different beast. Any AI guru will agree that knowledge acquisition and knowledge representation are two of their toughest challenges, and two of the most active areas of AI research. In this chapter we get right to the heart of expert systems and, as you can imagine, there are some daunting topics. We will barely scratch the surface.

To catch a first glimpse of the size of this challenge, let's look at some raw, unprocessed expertise right from the mouth of an expert. Here are some statements an experienced geologist might make about how to tell whether a particular site would be a good place to mine for a valuable ore he is seeking:

When you see the core samples taken from drilling in that rock formation, you will commonly find hematite ore. If you observe that the hematite has been substantially transformed into biotite, then that is a good indication that significant deposits of porphyry are present. And porphyry is the ore we are seeking as a source of molybdenum. But in at least a third of the cases, these core samples look promising, yet no commercial ore amounts are found. And of course we find porphyry without the biotite indicators. In that case . . .

This is the distillation of years of experience spilled out in a flurry of words.

To build an expert system, all this must be boiled down into "computer-friendly" statements like these:

If   hematite is found in concentrations of $\geq .30$
And   hematite has been $>50\%$ transformed into biotite
Then   conclude with a confidence level of .67 that commercial levels of porphyry are present.

And ultimately, the expert system must again be made "user-friendly" or else, just like any other software, it won't be used. This means that:

—The system must be easy to use by people who are neither leading experts in the field nor master computer programmers.

—It must give "good enough" conclusions to the type of problems that human experts are good at but that computers using conventional software can't handle.

—It can explain its reasoning to its users.

—The knowledge it contains can be upgraded, revised, and expanded.

—It does all this rapidly and efficiently.

Let's look at how all this happens. The first step is building the body of knowledge which goes into the expert system. This part of the process is called "knowledge acquisition."

KNOWLEDGE ACQUISITION: HOW AN EXPERT SYSTEM IS CREATED

Here is the ideal way to create an expert system: A leading expert in a particular field—let's say in diagnosing and treating cancer—decides he needs an expert system to advise him and other experts. So he sits down and writes out everything he knows about diagnosing and treating cancer. He also interviews other experts and culls information from all the major texts and medical journals. There is a vast amount of information, so this takes a lot of time and effort. Then he arranges all this expertise into a neat set of If-Then rules, and hires a programmer to encode all this into the computer. Lo and behold, he has an expert system! Thereafter, his diagnoses are much more consistent and accurate, and he gets rich from licensing his system to other doctors all over the world.

Every expert in the world must wish this were the case. Now, it's true there are expert system development tools that claim to guide any expert through just such a process. We used one in Chapter 3. However at their current stage of development they do not have an impressive track record for leading to successful commercial expert systems. The reality is that building an expert system takes extensive development time and effort. There are several reasons why, and we will discuss them in the next several sections.

Experts Can't Always Explain How They Solve Problems

What does an expert's knowledge consist of? Obviously it is much more than "book learning" the generally known concepts and facts about the problem area. From years of experience, experts have learned many tricks of the trade and shortcuts that never get into the books. Years of experience build their skills at spotting useful patterns and promising lines of inquiry among a confusing welter of input. They are skilled at forming hypotheses, testing and eliminating them, assigning likelihoods, making judgments and evaluations, and drawing conclusions. Their intuitive knowledge allows them to make good educated guesses that often cut right through to the solution. They have an overall understanding of the domain's problems and—just as important

—of what problems lie outside their domain of expertise. For the most part, this is the "heuristic" knowledge we described in Chapter 2.

But experts cannot easily explain how they solve problems. They often don't know the extent of their own knowledge. And they certainly do not know how to structure and arrange their knowledge so that it can be programmed into a computerized expert system. In many of the areas of expert systems, no single expert knows everything that is needed. Several experts' knowledge may have to be extracted and integrated. It may be difficult to get them together and impossible to keep them together for long enough. Beyond the standard book learning, they hold conflicting views, and may use incompatible problem-solving approaches.

A Knowledge Engineer Works With the Experts

Building expert systems has thus led to the emergence of a new kind of professional—the "knowledge engineer." The knowledge engineer is the one who actually builds the expert system by picking the brains of one or more specialists in the field who are called "domain experts," and programming the results into the computer. This is a very time-consuming, give-and-take process. Even after the initial set of facts has been assembled, the process of testing and refinement may take years. In the beginning, the knowledge engineer helps the experts express and clarify their thoughts. Typically, he will ask the experts to describe many examples and cases, and then work backward to derive axioms that embody the key knowledge.

Edward Shortliffe produced the Mycin program which diagnoses blood and meningitis infections and advises physicians on antibiotic therapies. His experience in incorporating the expertise of doctors Stanley Cohen and Stanton Axline provides a lesson in knowledge engineering:

> "We'd get together once a week and go over patient cases, and we would try to understand how Axline and Cohen would decide how to treat those cases," Shortliffe says. "We'd stop them—those of us who knew a little medicine and were more computer scientists—and ask, 'Well, why do you say that?'

Axline would have a patient's chart, and Cohen would try to figure out what he would do for that case, and we would try to understand why Cohen was asking the questions he was. We'd write down the rules that he would tell us, which Axline would help refine, and in the interim week I would put those rules into the emerging computer system."

Once enough rules were programmed into the computer, they would test its ability against known cases. Time after time it made stupid mistakes because it lacked some small piece of knowledge which humans take for granted as "common sense." So they continually added in background information to provide a context for interpreting the "expert" input. Correcting each omission and mistake turned out to take much longer than writing the initial set of rules.

"Plus," Shortliffe adds, "every once in a while some issues would arise which caused a major change in the underlying structure of the program." In this way the knowledge engineers become quite familiar with the problem domain themselves and begin to suggest new ways to tackle the problem that will work better for the computerized expert. To see this rule-building process more closely, let's zoom in on Session Number Umpteen of a "generic" knowledge engineering session, and listen to the knowledge engineer tease out the expert's knowledge. They are developing an expert system to help locate and cleanup the source of hazardous industrial waste spilled into a creek.

An Expert System to Advise in Cleaning Up Oil or Chemical Spills

K.E.: Suppose you were told that a spill had been detected in White Oak Creek one mile before it enters White Oak Lake. What would you do to contain the spill?

Exp.: That depends on a number of factors. I would need to find the source of the spill in order to prevent the possibility of further contamination, probably by checking drains and manholes for signs of the spill material. And it helps to know what the spilled material is.

K.E.: How can you tell what it is?

Exp.: Sometimes you can tell what the substance is by

its smell. Sometimes you can tell by its color, but that's not always reliable since dyes are used a lot nowadays. Oil, however, floats on the surface and forms a silvery film, while acids dissolve completely in the water. Once you discover the type of material spilled, you can eliminate any buildings that either don't store the material at all or don't store enough of it to account for the spill.

As this conversation continues, the knowledge engineer works out this prototype rule:

To determine spill material:
    [1] If the spill does not dissolve in water and the spill does form a silvery film, let the spill be oil.
    [2] If the spill does dissolve in water and the spill does form no film, let the spill be acid.
    [3] If the spill = oil and the odor of the spill is known, then choose situation: If the spill does smell of gasoline, let the material of the spill be gasoline with certainty .9; if the spill does smell of diesel oil, let the material of the spill be diesel oil with certainty .8.
    [4] If the spill = acid and the odor of the spill is known, then choose situation: If the spill does have a pungent/choking odor, let the material of the spill be hydrochloric acid with certainty .7; if the spill does smell of vinegar, let the material of the spill be acetic acid with certainty .8.
End

    K.E.: Here are some rules I think capture your explanation about determining the type of material spilled and eliminating possible spill sources. What do you think?
    Exp.: Uh-huh (long pause). Yes, that begins to capture it. Of course if the material is silver nitrate it will dissolve only partially in the water.
    K.E.: I see. Well, let's add that information to the knowledge base and see what it looks like.

The knowledge engineer has to add rules which embody the new information, and also revise the previous rules that will be affected by this change.

Add: Assert the solubility of the spill is [some level—high, moderate, low].

Delete: Assert the spill [does, does not] dissolve in water.

Modify: [1] If the solubility of the spill is low and the spill does form a silvery film, let the spill be oil.

Add: [1.5] If the solubility of the spill is moderate, let the material of the spill be silver nitrate with certainty .6.

Modify: [2] If the solubility of the spill is high and the spill does form no film, let the spill be acid.

The knowledge engineer and the expert continue to refine and expand the set of rules in this manner until they have enough to construct a workable prototype. They will check the accuracy and consistency of the rules with other experts. The prototype may take from several months up to a year to complete, and may contain several hundred rules and problem-solving guidelines.

At this stage, the prototype may become so unwieldy with rules and revisions from many different conversations and sources, that it is virtually unworkable. If so, the knowledge engineer may spend several more months rewriting and refining the rules before they have a workable prototype expert system with which they can begin field testing.

STAGES IN EXPERT SYSTEM DEVELOPMENT

Developing an expert system is clearly an "iterative" process, which means "design something, try it out, evaluate your results, redesign it, try it again, and so on until it works (or you run out of money and/or steam)." Developing an expert system involves several distinct though overlapping stages:

1. Define the Task

The knowledge engineer and the experts analyze the problem, first to determine whether it is appropriate for an expert system, and then to select a suitable general approach. They determine how large a

"Knowledge engineering"

bite of the problem to take. This may depend on the time and resources available for the project, especially the experts and the knowledge engineer. They will often define a small piece of the problem to
tackle first, both to test out some of the basic problem-solving strategies
to make sure they are on the right track, and to produce some initial
encouraging results to keep their spirits up (and to keep them funded).
For example, a goal may be to design an expert system that analyzes
the material of any hazardous spill; and a preliminary goal would be
reached when the system could determine if the material is oil-based.

2. Acquire the Knowledge and Problem-Solving Strategies

The knowledge engineer elicits the needed knowledge from one or more experts in the field. These experts identify the key concepts and facts and the ways they are linked together to solve problems.

3. Design the System

Formalize the knowledge into a set of rules, and build a structure to organize it. Program the rules into an AI language such as Lisp. Develop the kind of interface that its users will need.

4. Build and Test a Prototype Expert System

Test its performance against cases with known outcomes. Refine the rules.

5. Operate it

The expert system "graduates" and is used on real cases. Its results are doublechecked by its users.

6. Maintenance

Fine tuning, expanding its capabilities, and even major revision can continue indefinitely.

TOOLS FOR DEVELOPING
EXPERT SYSTEMS

Expert system development tools aid greatly in this process, easing some of the functions of the knowledge engineer. We will discuss some of these in Chapter 7. Even with such tools, however, each of the above-mentioned steps must be carefully attended to. If a professional knowledge engineer is not used, then the expert must fulfill that role himself. We are still a long way from the "ideal expert system generator" scenario above.

You can see that being a knowledge engineer takes a rare combination of skills. Besides being an expert at programming knowledge statements into the computer in an artificial intelligence language such as Lisp, the knowledge engineer must master enough of the specialist's field to ask intelligent questions and tell good answers from bad. He must also be able to deal with the impatience, frustration, and heartbreak when he runs into dead ends and when the system makes inexplicable errors. It is difficult, yet it is also very exciting and rewarding. The challenge and fun come from making sense out of a chaos of information and structuring knowledge in a way it has never before been expressed.

STEPS IN BUILDING AN EXPERT SYSTEM

Time Required

Identify the problem. Make sure it is appropriate for an expert system. Break it down into smaller pieces if possible.

Find the key knowledge concepts and problem-solving strategies the best experts use.

several months

Design an overall structure to organize the knowledge for efficient problem-solving

Put the knowledge and problem-solving strategies into rules, and encode them into computer language.

Test the prototype expert system against cases with known outcomes, and refine the rules.

6 months to 1 year

Operate the newly graduated expert system on real cases. Users doublecheck results.

Fine tuning, major revisions and expansions will continue idefinitely.

years

Refining and Upgrading the "Post-Graduate" Expert System

Eventually, the new expert system's performance rivals the performance of experts in the field. The initial problem for which it was designed is mastered. But this is not the end. The development team wants to expand its capabilities. New things emerge in its field. The team has to add new rules to handle these capabilities, and then conduct new tests to certify its expanded functions.

Often the expert system gets built up so much that it becomes unmanageable. Many different people have been working on it, and overlapping and contradictory rules get inserted. It needs a thorough redesign to make it more compact and efficient. This is by far the most time-consuming and expensive aspect of the expert system life-cycle. It is never-ending. As indicated in Figure 4–1, building the initial rule base and problem-solving structure may take several months, but fleshing this out to a workable prototype may take half a year, and refining it to expert-level performance may take a year or more. Then, for the rest of its life, it must be refined, upgraded, and redeveloped. Figure 4–1 shows the development time of several pioneering expert systems.

Actually, not all of the "classic" expert systems have undergone the redesign and redevelopment stage. The ones which have, such as Dendral and R1, are now commercially viable and are still being used in business or institutions. Others equally well-known and initially successful, such as Mycin, were not redesigned or expanded to handle new needs and are no longer used actively for their original purpose.

Why not? The viable ones have been picked up by a corporation or hospital or other program that depends on the system's efficient performance, and can provide the needed continuing support. Others, such as Mycin, never got out of the laboratory setting. Mycin's original team at Stanford has disbanded and gone on to new challenges. The university has a bias toward research, so there is less impetus and funding for the restructure of the expert system to the level of efficiency and comprehensiveness needed for commercial viability.

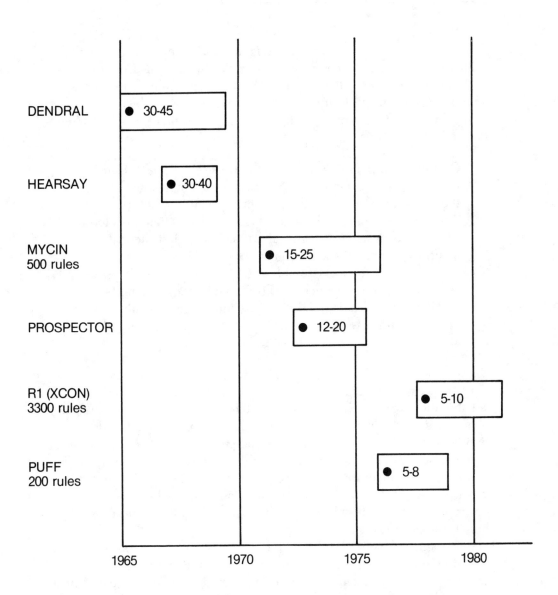

Figure 4–1
Development time and man-years of effort for some
expert systems

The Development of R1: A Successful Expert System

Here is an account of the development of R1, or XCON, the successful expert system used by Digital Equipment Corporation to configure the many pieces of computer hardware that are to be installed for a customer. It demonstrates the level of effort required to maintain a system's viability.

Why did DEC want an expert system in the first place? Stephen Polit at DEC tells us:

> Customers purchasing DEC computers may select from a wide variety of components; the problem is that some orders then contain combinations of pieces that will not operate together, and some orders lack essential components. Before XCON was designed, technical editors examined the orders, identified nonfunctional combinations of components, and provided instructions for assembling the system. Since this process caused a bottleneck at DEC, and many attempts to automate it had failed, DEC was willing to try to solve this problem with a technology that was relatively unexplored in an industrial setting.

The development of R1 began in December 1978 at Carnegie-Mellon University in Pittsburgh by John McDermott and several others, in collaboration with DEC. A set of initial capabilities was developed over the first four months. The knowledge acquired included descriptions of the most common DEC components R1 was to configure, and involved about 250 rules and a workable prototype. For the next six months R1's capabilities were refined by adding more component descriptions. By October 1979, R1 had 750 rules and 450 component descriptions, a system which stretched the capability of the computer being used.

In January 1980, CMU handed over this initial version to DEC, which immediately undertook a major rewrite of R1's rules, even going so far as to rewrite them in a different programming language and put the whole system on a larger computer. R1 emerged slimmed down from 750 to 500 rules and even more capable.

DEC formed a group of five people to continue R1's development. None had any prior AI background. (It is rumored that the name

"R1" came from a statement from one of its developers: "A month ago I couldn't even spell 'knowledge engineer' and now I R1.") Over the next four years, this group grew to seventy-seven people responsible for R1 and its offshoots. Initially, the group maintained a division of labor between those responsible for representing R1's knowledge as rules, and those who collected that knowledge. But after a couple of years, this distinction was pretty well broken down. The development group alternated between periods of broadening R1's capabilities and eliminating inadequacies in R1's knowledge and structure. This effort has taken about four man-years each year. R1's rule base has steadily grown as it has been programmed to configure new DEC systems and handle added functions during the configuration.

Figure 4–2 shows the rapid growth in the number of rules, from 850 by the end of 1980, to over 3500 by early 1984. In late 1984, R1 contained over 5500 component descriptions and could handle all of DEC's systems. R1 has been renamed XCON ("CON" for "configure") and has spawned several offspring: XSEL, a "seller's assistant" to help DEC sales representatives tailor a customer's order to his particular needs, and XSITE, which helps prepare a customer's site for the system's installation. DEC now relies heavily on R1 and continues its major commitment to keeping the system highly reliable.

In summary, there are three reasons why knowledge continues to be added to an expert system:

—To make minor refinements, such as adding knowledge to improve its performance on an existing task;

—To make major refinements, such as adding knowledge so it can perform a new task;

—To extend the definition of its central task in a significant way.

TWO CATEGORIES OF RULES: "KNOWLEDGE BASE" AND "INFERENCE ENGINE"

Throughout the knowledge acquisition process we have just described, the knowledge engineer separates emerging If-Then rules into two basic categories, the "knowledge base" and the "inference engine." Distinguishing and separating these two kinds of

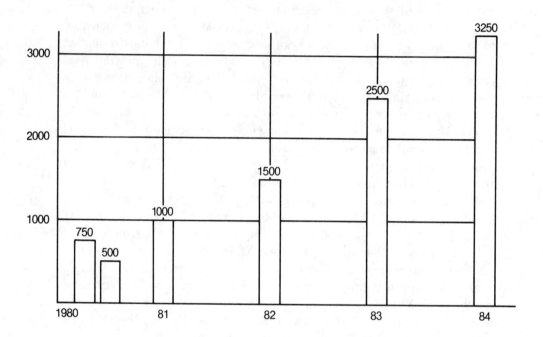

Figure 4–2
Growth in number of rules for R1

rules is a crucial feature of expert systems. First we will explain what the difference is, then we'll tell why separating them is so important.

Knowledge Rules and Inference Rules

Knowledge rules state all the facts and relationships about the problem, and inference rules tell you what to do with these facts to solve the problem.

Let's illustrate with a simple example. Suppose (heaven forbid!) that your personal computer bytes the dust. You turn it on, and it won't read your software in the disk drive. So you have to take it to the computer repairman. If he knows his stuff, he will know the facts about many different kinds of computers. But to work on any of them, he will follow a general troubleshooting plan. He will check the most obvious things first. Is it your software? Try another program. Is it your disk drive? Or is it in the computer itself? His tactic is to rule out quickly as many things as he can, and focus on the most likely problems. He starts from observed symptoms, and works backward to malfunctions which could cause them. If he's good, even after he locates one problem, he'll check for others, since he knows more than one thing can be wrong.

He will use this basic problem-solving strategy no matter what computer he is working on or what problem it has. He reasons his way through the problem, drawing on all the things he has learned. Any expert uses such a reasoning strategy. And so does any expert system. "Inferencing" is just a fancy word for "reasoning." So the expert's reasoning strategy becomes the expert system's inferencing strategy.

If he were an expert system, his *knowledge rules* would look like this:

> *If* customer's software program works in my disk drive, and it doesn't work in his disk drive,
>
> *Then* there is strong evidence that his disk drive is faulty.

His *inference rules*, on the other hand, would look like these:

> Begin by testing the part that is most closely associated with the reported symptoms.
>
> Conduct tests which will eliminate the greatest number of possible problems.
>
> If the first problem found doesn't account for all the symptoms, then test for other problems.

Full-fledged expert systems are obviously much more complex and detailed, but they all have the same two types of rules. Let's look briefly at how these are separated by the knowledge engineer, then see some actual examples from expert systems we are familiar with.

Separating Knowledge and Inference Rules

As the knowledge engineer draws out the crucial facts and relationships from his conversations with the domain expert, they are certainly not in any particular order. Figure 4–3 illustrates this process. At the top are rules derived from what the expert says. You could look at it as the unzipping of a zipper. The knowledge engineer unzips this seamless web of knowledge, with the knowledge rules on the left and the inference rules on the right. As the knowledge engineer separates the knowledge rules from the problem-solving strategy rules, he adds other inferencing rules from his own experience of how expert systems work. These go into the "buckets of rules" at the bottom. These buckets provide the raw material to construct the expert system. The knowledge rule bucket is organized into the knowledge base, and the inference engine is designed from the rules in the inference rule bucket.

Most of the rules we have seen up to now in this book have been knowledge rules from the knowledge bases of various expert systems. To make the distinction between knowledge base and inference engine clearer, let's again look at several familiar expert systems, and show examples of their knowledge and inference rules.

Mycin's Inferencing and Knowledge Rules

In the previous section, Mycin's creator recounted the process of developing Mycin. Here is the type of statement about how a doctor diagnoses an illness, which would be molded into inference engine rules:

> After I observe the patient and look at the initial data, I can immediately rule out most possible diseases. I typically take the condition which seems most likely and look for evidence which would tend to prove its existence. This way I quickly discover what further tests I need to provide the corroborating evidence. After that, if there is not enough evidence to support my first hypothesis, or if I find evidence which disproves it, then I'll set it aside and consider something else.

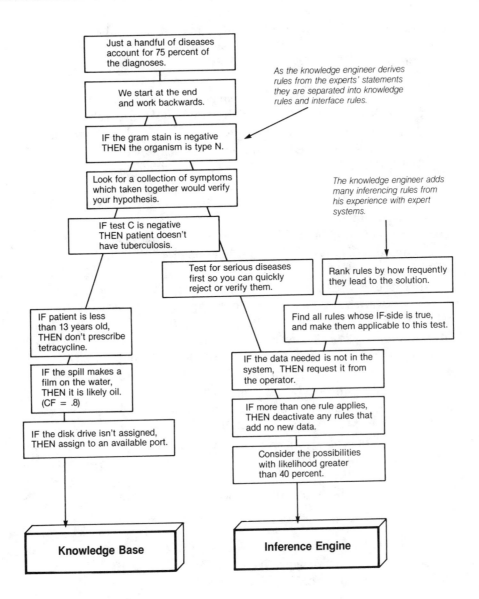

As the knowledge engineer derives rules from the experts' statements they are separated into knowledge rules and interface rules.

Just a handful of diseases account for 75 percent of the diagnoses.

We start at the end and work backwards.

IF the gram stain is negative THEN the organism is type N.

Look for a collection of symptoms which taken together would verify your hypothesis.

The knowledge engineer adds many inferencing rules from his experience with expert systems.

IF test C is negative THEN patient doesn't have tuberculosis.

Test for serious diseases first so you can quickly reject or verify them.

Rank rules by how frequently they lead to the solution.

IF patient is less than 13 years old, THEN don't prescribe tetracycline.

Find all rules whose IF-side is true, and make them applicable to this test.

IF the spill makes a film on the water, THEN it is likely oil. (CF = .8)

IF the data needed is not in the system, THEN request it from the operator.

IF the disk drive isn't assigned, THEN assign to an available port.

IF more than one rule applies, THEN deactivate any rules that add no new data.

Consider the possibilities with likelihood greater than 40 percent.

Knowledge Base

Inference Engine

Figure 4–3
The knowledge engineer divides the emerging expertise into knowledge base rules and inference rules, and adds his own inference rules. The knowledge rules become the knowledge base and the inference rules become the inference engine.

A statement like this becomes a central part of the control strategy of an expert system like Mycin. This problem-solving strategy would then be applied to all diagnostic situations for which that expert system is used.

1) **From the facts of the case, select a candidate diagnosis.**
2) **Work backwards through rules which link observable conditions with a particular diagnosis, and seek a diagnosis which is supported by the evidence of the case.**
3) **If more data is needed, request it from the system's operator.**
4) **Explore all possible diagnoses, then rank them according to likelihood.**
5) **Recommend an antibiotic treatment which is appropriate for the diagnoses with high likelihood.**

Because Mycin's inference engine starts with a conclusion and works backwards to seek supporting evidence, its inference strategy is called *backward reasoning* or *backward chaining*. This notion is related to the old idea of "reverse engineering." If there is just too much data to start from where you are and chug through to the right solution, then pick a likely solution and work backwards from it, to see if it works out. If it does work, you have solved the problem; and if it doesn't, then try another one until you find one which does work. We'll see how Mycin does this in Chapter 5. Now for contrast, let's look again at one of Mycin's knowledge base rules, like the ones we have seen previously.

If   1) the gram stain of the organism is gram negative, and
            2) the morphology of the organism is rod, and
            3) the aerobicity of the organism is anaerobic,
Then   there is suggestive evidence (.7) that the identity
            of the organism is Bacteroides.

As we said before, Mycin has about 500 knowledge rules like this, pertaining to many infectious blood diseases and the conditions which relate to them. It is these rules that are examined, using Mycin's inference strategy, to reach a conclusion about the disease and the best drug treatment.

Dendral's Knowledge and Inference Rules.

Dendral, you recall, helps chemists find the structure of unknown molecules. Here is the kind of statement a chemist might have made when Dendral was being developed:

> Since we can't directly determine by lab tests the shape of a newly-discovered organic molecule, and there are millions of possible structures, we will first drastically narrow the number of possibilities by studying the compound's X-ray diffraction pattern. Now we know that certain diffraction patterns correlate with certain shapes. After we eliminate the ones we know cannot work, we then pick the most likely shapes and test them one at a time until we find the best fit.

Statements like these were painstakingly crafted into a set of inference rules which, taken together, form Dendral's inference engine. Here is its basic inference strategy:

1. **Examine the data from chemical analysis of the substance under consideration to eliminate unlikely molecular structures, and to establish constraints for its structure.**

Figure 4–4
The inference engine, fueled by knowledge rules, chugs through
the data to reach the conclusion

2. Use rules in the knowledge base to generate a candidate molecular structure which fits these constraints.
3. Use the rules in the knowledge base for predicting a molecule's spectrograph from its structure and predict the mass spectrograph for the candidate structure.
4. Compare this predicted structure with the data from chemical analysis, to see if it is consistent.
5. Repeat this process until a structure is found that fits the data.

This inference strategy is called "generate and test." It generates a hypothesis, then tests it against the data. Since there are initially millions of possibilities, this works only because the rules from the knowledge base have allowed the number of alternatives which fit the constraints to be drastically limited in the first step. We'll say more about this in Chapter 5.

Here is an example of Dendral's knowledge rules, which its inference engine uses to find a molecular structure:

If   the mass spectrum shows data points at masses $x(1)$ and $x(2)$ such that the sum of $x(1)$ and $x(2)$ is the molecular weight plus 28 mass units (the overlapping $C=0$ group) and at least one of the two peaks is high (because the fragmentation is favorable)

Then   infer that the molecular structure contains the subgraph

$$\overset{\text{\O}}{\underset{R1-C-R2}{\mid}}$$

where the masses of R1 and R2 are just $(x(1) - 28)$ and $(x(2) - 28)$.

This rule allows chemists to interpret the molecular structure of an organic compound and the locations of particular pieces around its skeleton.

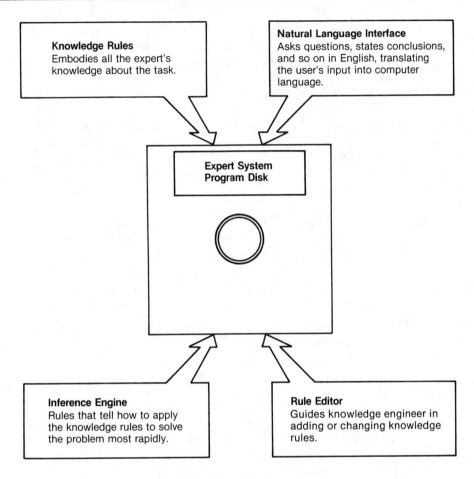

Figure 4–5
What goes into the expert system program

R1 or XCON's Inference and Knowledge Rules.

For one last example, let's recall R1 from Chapter 2, which configures VAX computer systems. R1's inference strategy is to break configuration task down into 6 subtasks and solve each one in order:

1. **Correct any mistakes in the customer's order.**
2. **Put components into central processing unit cabinets.**
3. **Put boxes into unibus cabinets and put components in boxes.**

4. **Put panels in unibus cabinets.**
5. **Lay out the system on the customer's floor plan.**
6. **Design the cabling which will connect all the components.**

For each subtask, R1 makes definite matches based on the data from the order, the descriptions of components it has stored, and rules for proper combinations and arrangements of components. Thus its inference strategy is called "data driven matching" or "forward chaining." We will contrast forward and backward chaining in Chapter 5. While going through this inference strategy, R1 can draw on about 3300 rules, of which this is one:

> *If*   the current subtask is assigning devices to unibus modules and there is an unassigned dual port disk drive and the type of controller it requires is known and there are two such controllers, neither of which has any devices assigned to it and the number of devices which these controllers can support is known
>
> *Then*   assign the disk drive to each controller and note that each controller supports one device.

The Inference Strategy Must Fit the Task

You can see that these expert systems use quite varied approaches to their tasks. They emulate the way the human experts tackle these problems. In Chapter 5, we will come back to this and show how the characteristics of the problem shape the inference strategy.

KNOWLEDGE RULES ARE SEPARATED FROM INFERENCING RULES TO MAKE UPDATING THE EXPERT SYSTEM EASIER

As we demonstrated above, expert systems are never finished, so it is essential that they can be easily updated. Separating the knowledge base from the inference engine allows revision of one rule with a minimum impact on the other rules.

An expert system is composed almost entirely of *If-Then* rules, which can be plucked out, added, or changed, without restructuring the rest of the expert system program. You'll see in Chapter 6 how this works, and how it is different from reprogramming conventional software programs. As we saw in the knowledge acquisition examples above, this allows debugging, correcting errors in rules, and expanding the system's capabilities.

By keeping the knowledge rules separate, the domain expert can focus on the areas of his expertise, and not be concerned with the problem-solving mechanism in the inference engine. Once the expert's basic problem-solving strategy is clarified and programmed into the inference engine, it is much more important for him to focus on refining the knowledge rules, and leave the knowledge engineer to polish the rules for interpreting and controlling the system.

The knowledge base rules are more likely to need changing than are the inference engine rules. This may seem surprising, since the inferencing rules were harder to clarify initially. It was hard for the experts to say how they solve problems. Yet once stated clearly and built into the system, the problem-solving and inferencing rules remain quite stable.

The knowledge base rules, on the other hand, are always being changed. In the first place, the knowledge rule cannot be stated completely and correctly on the first pass. That's in the nature of the task. If you could do so, you would be dealing with a task which didn't need an expert system. Second, the users always want to expand the system's capabilities and its areas of usefulness. And third, the information in the field changes. The rules must be modified to reflect those changes. And finally, as the expert system is used, its users gain experience which allows them to state the facts and relationships more accurately. So, as we saw with R1, a rule must be added here, another deleted there, and some of the remaining ones changed, both to reflect an evolving understanding of the processes involved, and to allow the expert system to take on more tasks.

To sum up, building an expert system is a tinkerer's dream. If the rules can't be changed quite easily, no one will make the effort for long to keep them updated, and the system will stagnate and die from obsolescence. This ability to update and change rules easily depends on two things: having the knowledge base rules separated from the inference rules, and using a structure and programming language which makes it possible to change rules with minimum impact on the remaining rules. We will say more about that in Chapter 6.

Extracting the Inference Engine

One of the most interesting features of expert systems follows from this separation of inference engine from knowledge base. Knowledge engineers quickly discovered that they could remove *all* the knowledge rules, leaving only the inferencing and controlling rules. Into this isolated inference engine, they could plug an entire new set of knowledge rules, and have a whole new expert system for some completely different task. For example, they could remove all the human disease diagnostic rules from Mycin, and plug in rules for diagnosing malfunctions in automobiles. And it worked! This feature has greatly aided the more rapid development of later generations of expert systems. We'll show you all about it in Chapter 7. But before that, in the next chapter we'll show you how the inference engine chews through the knowledge rules to reach the conclusion.

CHAPTER 5

SEARCHING THROUGH KNOWLEDGE FOR ANSWERS

- **Heuristic Search Strategies**
- **Forward and Backward Reasoning with Rules**
- **Decision Trees**

You have now seen many individual knowledge rules and inference rules from several expert systems. In this chapter, we will see how an expert system puts all these rules together to solve a problem. The way an expert system applies its knowledge rules is called its heuristic search strategy. Every expert system has a general problem-solving strategy, built into the rules in its inference engine, that searches through all its knowledge rules and all the data available until it finds a pattern that leads to a solution. This is called a heuristic strategy because the rules that guide the search are derived from the informal rules of thumb used by experts in the field.

It shouldn't surprise us that an expert system that diagnoses diseases uses an approach similar to that used by successful doctors. It's instructive to realize that the computer experts have so far been unable to come up with general problem-solving strategies that work even as well as those we humans use.

Experts in different fields, of course, use different approaches to their tasks. These approaches have been built up through the experience of many people and are presumably among the most efficient and effective way to tackle the particular tasks at hand. The expert system for each task is based on the approach that human experts have found most effective. Thus, there is no such thing as a "generic" expert system. The tool must be designed to fit the task. We will look at how several expert systems that use different search strategies search through their rules to see why each uses the particular strategy it does. To gain an understanding of two of the most common expert system search strategies, let's first pursue some fanciful searches that illustrate some of the basic issues involved.

1. THE FORWARD REASONING TREASURE HUNTER

Suppose you are hunting hidden treasure. You've long heard the legend of the pirate gold hidden in a cave called "La Boca del Diablo" somewhere in a bay along the north coast of South America, a coast full of bays and caves.

This story was only legend until you found a scrap of map in an antique dresser in a little shop in Caracas. Parts of the map were missing, but there were enough clues to get you started. The scrap shows a coastline, a compass rose, a drawing of a cave entrance that looks like an open mouth, and the scrawled initials LJS—Long John Silver, the pirate who hid the gold! Legend says that Long John hid his treasure along the north coast of South America. Because the map looks like this:

LA BOCA
DEL DIABLO

you deduce that the bay faces east. Putting these two pieces of information together, you deduce that the treasure must be hidden in an east-facing bay along a generally north-facing coast. A search of a modern map narrows this down to three sections of coast.

An old Spanish novel based on the diaries of one of Long John's sailors describes the sections of coast they sailed each year, so you can state these rules:

> If the year is 1791, then they sailed coast section A.
> If the year is 1792, then they sailed section B.
> If the year is 1793, then they sailed section C.
> If the year is 1794, then they sailed section D.
>
> If coast section A, then bays M, N, and O face east.
> If coast section B, then no bays face east. Reject coast B.
> If coast section C, then bays P and Q face east.
> If coast section D, then bay R faces east.

To narrow this list down further, you must find information on the year the treasure was buried. From old port logs in Cartegeña, you find that the treasure was stolen in 1791. Thus you have evidence that the cave is in bay M, N, or O. There are many caves in these bays, and none are currently called "Mouth of the Devil." How do you decide where to search? You have rules like this:

> If the bay is suitable for hiding a pirate ship, then there is evidence the treasure cave is in that bay.

By sailing along these three bays, you find that only one can be sailed into safely. You sail in and look for cave entrances, photographing all that you find. Now it is time to "generate and test." That is, you rank the caves by how closely they resemble a devil's mouth, then explore them one at a time until—success!—you find the one with the chest of gold buried within.

Dendral Uses Forward Reasoning

This approach is quite similar to the one Dendral uses to discover the structure of an organic compound. Here are some of the similarities. We know in general what we are looking for: location of the cave with the treasure, or the structure of an unknown chemical. Our rules are derived from our general expertise and are tested against the facts of the situation. We don't, however, have all the facts at first. The facts we find by applying the rules at each stage do two things for us: One, they help us eliminate some of the possible outcomes from further consideration and, two, they point out places where we need further information to move forward to the next level. For example, once we found out the treasure was stolen in 1791, we could eliminate from consideration all coasts the pirates sailed in other years. Similarly, once Dendral knows that a compound has certain characteristics, it eliminates from consideration any compounds that don't fit that pattern.

Some paths are quickly eliminated. We seek ways to narrow the search as rapidly as possible. The key to successful heuristic search is to eliminate unlikely paths of search as rapidly as possible. The treasure hunter could search through every bay seeking the treasure cave, but this would make the search prohibitively lengthy and expensive. Likewise with Dendral, which has literally millions of possibilities to consider. In both cases, the data is incomplete and uncertain. You can't be sure of any of your conclusions until you find the gold. The rules and data you have may not lead to the treasure, but if you find it, you are certain you have reached your goal. Dendral shares another feature of your treasure hunt: All input is not verbal or natural language. Data for Dendral and some other systems are partly graphic representations, similar to your treasure map.

2. THE BACKWARD REASONING DETECTIVE

Let's now contrast the approach you used to find Long John's Treasure with a situation in which you would use backward reasoning to reach a solution most efficiently. Imagine you are a renowned private eye working on the sensational murder of a world-famous computer manufacturer. Who would commit such a dastardly deed? You are confronted with a baffling variety of clues that seem to point to many people the victim knew.

But then you say, "Really, there are just a few people who could have done this. I'll consider them one at a time and work backward to the clues. First, suppose the butler did it. If he did, then I would expect to discover certain things about him." As an expert detective, you have standard rules you can use to test against each suspect. You know that even if a person satisfies all the conditions of a rule, it is not certain that he committed the crime. You assign a "seat-of-the-pants" likelihood (or unlikelihood) depending on your judgment of how strong the evidence is:

> If a person gains substantially from victim's death;
> If a person fears a serious loss from the victim;
> If a person is linked to someone else with a motive;
> If a person is linked to the murder weapon;
> Or if there is evidence of unscrupulous behavior;
> Then he is a murder suspect.

> If a person has no motive;
> If a person has a sound alibi;
> Then he is *unlikely* as a murder suspect.

You can thus determine, "The butler seems to have no motive and has a good alibi, so I can rule him out as a likely suspect. I conclude that the butler did not murder him." You continue: "Perhaps his secretary did it. If she did, I would expect to find certain things." But the evidence here is inconclusive. You may decide to investigate further to collect more evidence, and now you know more precisely what you should look for. But for now you continue with your plan to consider each suspect in turn.

Next you consider the victim's partner. You figure that the partner would stand to gain financially from the murder, but you can't find any direct way he would benefit. You look for indirect evidence. With some checking, you find that a large block of the computer company's stock is owned by a holding company, and that the partner owns 25 percent of that stock. His control of the computer firm thus increases substantially with the other partner's death. Aha! This and other clues point to him. You match the new data with more of the tacit rules you have built up from your experience with similar cases:

> If the partner owns 25 percent of the holding company, then there is evidence that he would gain financially from victim's death.

If the partner feared victim was trying to edge him out, then
he felt threatened with loss by victim.

You can build a pretty strong case against the partner, even
though there are some loose ends. You could stop here, but you
decide to consider several other people. You consider the victim's
ex-wife. You check her motives against the rules and against certain
pieces of evidence, and again things click. Now you have two suspects.
Which one did it? Some added inquiries reveal that the ex-wife also
owns 25 percent of the holding company stock. Perhaps she and the
partner were in cahoots! And then you find that they had both charged
tickets to Acapulco at almost the same time . . .

If she is linked to someone else with a motive;
If she shows evidence of unscrupulous behavior . . .

You actually have a stronger case against them now than if you had
been satisfied with the first good answer. You now decide not to
consider anyone else, because your conclusion—although not 100 percent certain—is good enough.

Mycin Uses Backward Reasoning

This is quite similar to the way that Mycin and other backward-
reasoning expert systems work. They start with a best guess and then
quickly try to eliminate unlikely answers to narrow the field. They
work backward through predetermined decision-guiding rules to see
which suspects best match the evidence. They often require more than
one step to make this match, so they must work backward through
their rules.

When they come to a question they cannot answer, they request
further information. The unfulfilled *if* sides of the rules guide the
asking of questions that lead to new facts. New rules are suggested by
the facts and connections that emerge. These rules are added to the
rule base for future cases. Even when these expert systems cannot get
all the information they need, they make the best conclusions they can
with the information they have, and they rank conclusions according to
their likelihood. They do more than reach "yes" or "no" decisions.

Many expert systems, including Mycin, search systematically through all suspects. They know that there can be more than one answer, and that it is important to find all of them. Other systems learn to stop when they reach a conclusion that is "good enough."

Why the Different Strategies?

The detective and the treasure hunter each use a different heuristic search strategy, and each has a good reason. The seeker of hidden treasure uses forward reasoning. She starts with a set of clues and works forward step by step. At each stage she discovers new clues and narrows the number of possible locations. At last only one location remains. The detective, on the other hand, uses backward reasoning. He starts by considering a few of the most likely murder suspects and then works backwards to see which one best matches the available clues. "For it to be the butler, I would expect to find a motive, the means, and the lack of a good alibi. Do I find these?"

Could the treasure seeker use backward reasoning? Could she start by testing a particular goal against the clues? In her case, this would mean checking every nook and cranny along the coast of South America to see which looked like the place on the map. A daunting task! What about the detective? Couldn't he just start with the clues at hand and see where they led? With some investigations, this is the best way. But in this case, the clues were ambiguous and elusive. He didn't even know what all the clues were. It may become apparent that seemingly disconnected facts are useful clues only in the context of investigating a particular suspect.

These two approaches to searching parallel the two most common search strategies used by expert systems: forward chaining strategies and backward chaining strategies. Mycin is an example of a backward chaining expert system, and Dendral and R1 are examples of forward chaining systems.

Chaining: Reasoning by Linking Rules Together

Why is reasoning called *chaining*? Expert systems reason in complex situations by linking together—or chaining—a number of their knowledge-based rules. Some reason backward like the detective, and

Backward chaining expert systems, such as Mycin, start by selecting a likely solution. and working backward to find evidence which will confirm or disprove it.

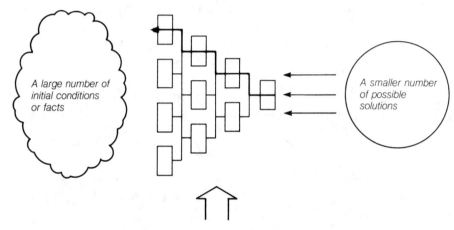

A large number of initial conditions or facts

A smaller number of possible solutions

The decision tree of rules used to prune the number of alternatives to consider

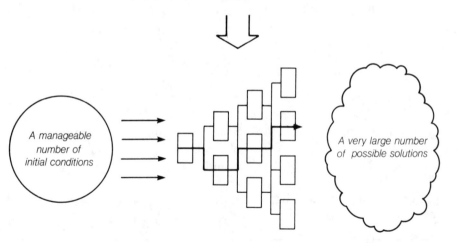

A manageable number of initial conditions

A very large number of possible solutions

Forward chaining expert systems, such as Dendral, start with a small set of facts, and use their rules to work toward the best answer.

In either case, the system starts where there is the smallest number of things to consider initially.

**Figure 5–1
When backward and forward chaining are used**

COMPARING FORWARD AND BACKWARD CHAINING

BACKWARD CHAINING	FORWARD CHAINING
"Given a question, try to answer it."	"Given a situation, try to respond to it."
Start by suggesting a possible solution to a problem, and then working backward to see if it is correct.	Start from the data given and work forward to a solution which is consistent with it.
Test the hypothesis against the data available to see if the evidence supports it.	Examine the data available to find constraints which will limit the search.
Ask questions to seek data which will prove or disprove the hypothesis.	Apply the rules to generate plausible alternative conclusions. Predict the best outcome, and compare the prediction to the data to find the best fit.
Can explain its reasoning.	Does not explain its reasoning.
Tries to minimize the number of questions asked.	Tries to minimize the number of irrelevant possible solutions examined.
Also called "top down" or "goal driven" reasoning.	Also called "bottom up" or "data driven" reasoning.

their search strategy is called *backward chaining*. Other systems reason forward, like the treasure hunter, and their strategy is called *forward chaining*. We'll see how some expert systems do this, but let's first look at the chaining of rules by examining a simplified version of a could-be expert system.

Forward Chaining Auto Diagnosis

Suppose you get into your car one fine morning, turn the key in the ignition, and the car won't start. The engine turns over, but the car doesn't start. Since you are a semi-expert mechanic, you don't immediately go into panic mode or call the automobile club. You apply your experience and start troubleshooting to find the problem. You start with the facts you can observe, draw conclusions about what they mean, ask questions and check things out, step by step, until you identify the problem and determine how to remedy it. Figure 5–2 shows a map of all the rules you could apply to solve the problem. You are eager to get to work, and want your car started quickly, so you want to work through your troubleshooting map as rapidly as possible (remember Chapter 2's combinatorial explosion).

Here's what you do at each step: Take an action, observe the result, and depending on the result, take one action or another. In this way you are guided through the sequence of steps in the map. If this were an expert system that diagnoses automobile malfunctions, each of these tests would be built into a rule, and the map in Figure 5–2 would contain those rules from the system's knowledge base that pertain to the problem you are trying to solve, arranged in the order in which you must test them. Such a map is called a decision tree. At each branch of the decision tree, you will be guided next to one rule or another, depending on the result of the test there. Here are the rules you would consider:

If turning on ignition key doesn't start the engine,
Then observe whether engine turns over.

If engine turns over without starting,
Then check gas gauge.

If gas gauge indicates sufficient gasoline,
Then smell for odor of gasoline.

If engine turns over without starting,
Then check for loose wires to spark plugs and coil.

If engine turns over without starting
And no wires are loose,
Then check coil for color of spark.

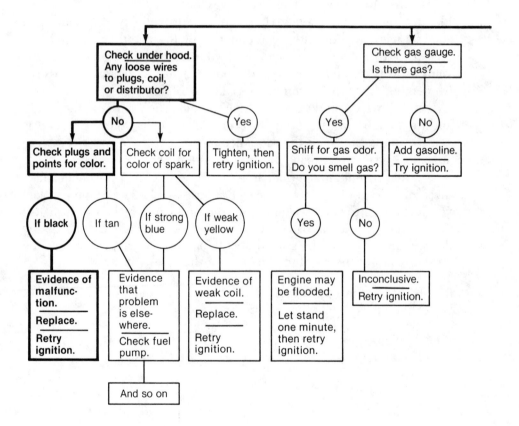

Figure 5–2
Decision tree for forward chaining auto troubleshooter

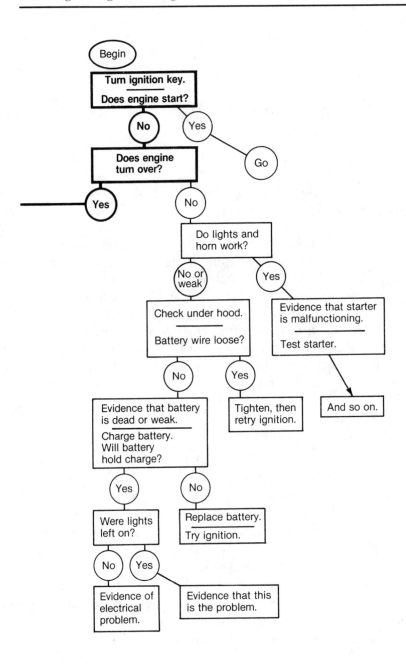

If coil's spark is bright blue-white,
Then coil is okay.

If coil's spark is dim yellow,
Then coil needs to be replaced.

If coil needs to be replaced,
Then check spark plugs and points also.

If spark plugs are black and dirty,
Then spark plugs are misfiring.

And so on until you conclude resignedly that your tuneup can be postponed no longer. There goes your trip to the lake!

Many expert systems work in just this way. Each rule tested requires that the user supply some further data. The outcome of testing one rule leads to the next one along the chain. To discover the problem, the system goes through an entire chain of rules, and this is why this process is called chaining. Because the process followed here starts with some initial conditions and works forward through the rules to reach the solution, it is called "forward chaining."

Strategies for Efficient Searching

When your car didn't start, you didn't test every rule. You were guided along one chain of rules—the ones highlighted—until you found the problem and its solution. Likewise with an expert system: In any one problem-solving session, only a fraction of its knowledge rules are brought into play.

There are several important general observations to make about this testing process that apply to expert systems as well. These rules could be checked in many different sequences and presumably would lead you to the same conclusion. But if you are a good mechanic, you learn through experience to find the quickest and most reliable ways to reach the solution.

You immediately check the gas gauge and try the lights and horn. Likewise, an expert system first conducts those tests that can lead immediately to a solution or can quickly eliminate a significant possibility. You ignore the possibility that the gas gauge may be broken, because in the past it has proven reliable. Likewise an expert system knows how frequently a particular test leads to a solution. It first runs those tests that most often lead to the solution, and leaves until later those that seldom do. You combine tests whenever you can. While you check under the hood for loose battery wires, you check for loose spark plug wires at the same time. Expert systems also combine tests in this manner. You choose a strategy for conducting tests depending on the problem you are trying to solve. You can either conduct several top level tests first, before going on to any deeper tests, or you can test one system thoroughly before going on to another system. We could first test the rule at the top of each branch before going on to any rule down the branch. With our car, we could check the rules along the top: horns and lights, gas gauge, and spark plug wires before moving down any branch. This is called a "breadth-first" test.

Or we could test all the rules vertically down one branch before moving horizontally across the decision tree to test any rules at the top of the chain. Here we might check all the rules under "horn and lights" before checking even the gas gauge. This is called a "depth-first" search strategy. An expert system adopts whichever strategy will lead most rapidly to the solution of the problem. Our troubleshooter combines breadth-first and depth-first for efficiency. He first checks both the gas gauge and the horn and lights, and then, depending on what was discovered, selects the branch to work down.

THE TROUBLESHOOTER'S INFERENCE ENGINE

All the rules we have mentioned for search strategy in an expert system are contained in the inference engine. At each step, the inference engine of our troubleshooter—like a backseat driver—is giving instructions.

—**"First make all the easy tests."**
—**"Did one test point to a problem? Good. Now conduct the next test down that branch."**

—"Negative result? OK, then go back up to the top of the next branch and conduct that test."

—"Found a solution which accounts for all the symptoms? All right, state the conclusion."

Each time one of the knowledge rules is selected or tested or set aside, it is one of the inference rules guiding this process.

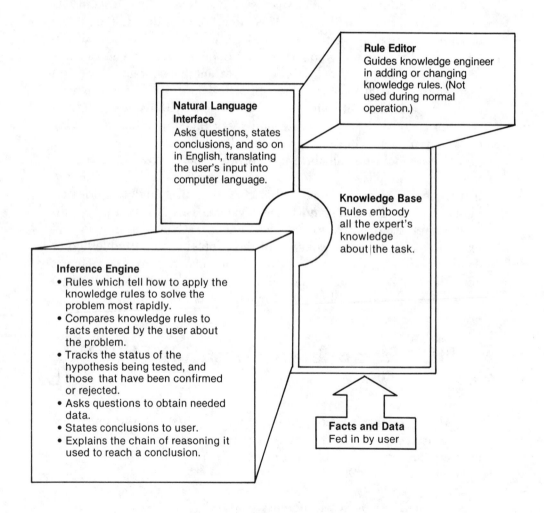

Rule Editor
Guides knowledge engineer in adding or changing knowledge rules. (Not used during normal operation.)

Natural Language Interface
Asks questions, states conclusions, and so on in English, translating the user's input into computer language.

Knowledge Base
Rules embody all the expert's knowledge about the task.

Inference Engine
• Rules which tell how to apply the knowledge rules to solve the problem most rapidly.
• Compares knowledge rules to facts entered by the user about the problem.
• Tracks the status of the hypothesis being tested, and those that have been confirmed or rejected.
• Asks questions to obtain needed data.
• States conclusions to user.
• Explains the chain of reasoning it used to reach a conclusion.

Facts and Data
Fed in by user

Figure 5–3
The expert system, focusing on the inference engine

The System's Limits

There are possibilities that aren't covered in these rules. For example, your engine could cough and sputter, then die. Your starter might make a clicking sound. A good mechanic notices any such additional symptoms, and has learned strategies for solving new problems. There could also be more than one problem. You could replace your spark plugs and assume you had solved the problem, only to discover later that your points are also bad. Diagnostic expert systems must also have rules that allow them to discover multiple problems and to know when several problems may be linked. For example, if you haven't had a tuneup for 15,000 miles, there is a good chance that your plugs and points both need to be changed. But an expert system would not notice this unless it has been specifically programmed to do so. An expert system doesn't learn new rules and tests by itself, but as we have seen before, it is built so that its users can easily update it with new facts. But at present, expert systems are not very good at recognizing when problems are outside the expertise built into their rule bases.

Backward-Chaining Mycin-Style Diagnosis

Let's look behind the scenes at a typical diagnostic session. This is similar to a Mycin session, but it is simplified to point out the main feature of a backward-chaining system better. We'll call it Unmycin. We'll see how Unmycin goes through its rules, evaluates the data fed into it by the doctor using it, and reaches a conclusion. Unmycin, like Mycin, is a backward-chaining system, and like Mycin, its knowledge has three kinds of rules.

1. **Rules to help reveal the identities of organisms causing disease that use the characteristics of organisms**
2. **Rules that use laboratory data to help discover the characteristics of the organisms.**
3. **Rules that then use the identity of the disease-causing organisms and the individual characteristics of the patient to help find the best drug treatment.**

Here is a rule from Mycin that combines 1 and 2:

> *If*   a) the gram stain of the organism is gram negative, and
> b) the morphology of the organism is rod, and
> c) the aerobicity of the organism is anaerobic,
>
> *Then*   there is suggestive evidence (.7) that the identity of the organism is Bacteroides.

Here are the steps Unmycin goes through in putting these rules together during a diagnostic session:

1. Select the bacteria to test first. The patient is suffering from a serious case of the dreaded lurgy, an infection which could be caused by any of several bacterial agents, including bug-eyed germs or beady-eyed germs. Suppose Unmycin decides to test first for bug-eyed germs.

2. Find the rules pertaining to bug-eyed germs. Unmycin looks through its 500 rules and finds all those that draw a conclusion about bug-eyed germs, and passes over those that do not. For example:

Testing for bug-eyed germs:

RULE

| A | IF | Test for Antibody A is positive | THEN | there is weak evidence for bug-eyed germs (.2) |

| B | IF | Germ has shape: Bulbous | THEN | there is suggestive evidence for bug-eyed germs (.4) |
| | AND | Germ has character: large eyes | | |

| C | IF | Germ has shape: Skinny | THEN | there is suggestive evidence for beady-eyed germs (.5) |
| | AND | Germ has character: tiny eyes | | |

| D | IF | Patient has symptom: yellowish skin cast | THEN | there is suggestive evidence for bug-eyed germs (.6) |
| | AND | Patient doesn't have hepatitis | | |

. . . and so on. Unmycin selects Rules A, B, and D to test and rejects Rule C because it says nothing about bug-eyed germs. It stores the three selected rules in its internal working memory.

3. Compare These Rules to the Data. Mycin then examines the *If*-side of each of these selected rules and compares their premises to the initial data of the case. For each premise, it seeks a match; it asks the question: Do the facts match the premise? For example:

INITIAL DATA ENTERED BY DOCTOR	IF-SIDES OF RULES WHICH CONCLUDE ABOUT BUG-EYED GERMS		
Patient's age: 38	A	IF	Test for Antibody A is positive
Sex: M			
Medical history:	B	IF	Germ has shape: Bulbous
—		AND	Germ has character: large eyes
—			
Results of lab tests:	D	IF	Patient has symptom: yellowish skin cast
—			
—			
Observed symptoms:		AND	Patient doesn't have hepatitis
Yellowish skin cast			
—			

If it finds a match between the data fed in by the doctor and the *If* side of one of the rules it is considering, as shown for Rule D above, then that also confirms Rule D with a certain likelihood. That is, since the data says "patient has symptom: yellowish skin cast," then it suggests with a likelihood of .4 that bug-eyed germs are present.

4. Seek confirming data from the doctor. Next, Unmycin looks again at the *If*-side of the other rules it is considering, and asks the doctor questions that would bring out confirming or negating evidence for those rules. It might ask:

```
Did you find that germ has shape: bulbous?
Does Bug have character: large eyes?
```

Here's how Unmycin asks such questions. Built into it are phrases like, "Did you find. . . ?" and "Does bug have. . . ?" which are activated by the system's decision that it needs more data to reach a conclusion. It attaches these phrases to the appropriate part of the *If*-side of the rule that it is testing. In the doctor's responses to these questions, the yes and no answers are equally important.

5. Reach a conclusion if possible. If enough data is available at this point, Unmycin can reach a conclusion about bug-eyed germs with a high level of confidence. But if not, which is most often the case, then it resurveys its knowledge rules and finds all the rules whose *Then*-sides state a conclusion about the data the system has just requested. For example, if Rule E says:

Rule

E   If symptom swelling of the   THEN there is evidence for bug-
     spleen is found   eyed germs (.5).

then Unmycin would ask the doctor:

    Did you find swelling of the spleen?

The doctor can answer yes, no, or not known. If the doctor is certain that swelling of the spleen is not present, and answers "No," then according to Rule E2, the corollary of Rule E:

E2   If symptom swelling of   THEN bug-eyed germs are very
     the spleen is absent   unlikely.

In this case, Unmycin would reject its hypothesis that bug-eyed germs are causing the dreaded lurgy, and begin checking for beady-eyed germs.

If the doctor answers "Yes" to the question, then Unmycin concludes that there is a 50 percent likelihood that bug-eyed germs are present. But let's assume he answers "Not known." Then Unmycin must go to another level of rules. This is where backward chaining comes in.

6. Backward chaining to seek confirming evidence. Oftentimes, the necessary additional data is not available. For example, the data needed to determine the presence of bug-eyed germs might require the results of a lab test that takes 48 hours to develop. Doctors often

face this situation, but they can't wait. Serious infection can cripple or kill a patient in that time. So they have learned to spot preliminary indicators of lab test results.

This knowledge has also been incorporated into Unmycin as a set of rules that gives the doctor a good indication. In a sense, these rules are built into Unmycin in layers. The *Then*-side of the second layer of rules draws a conclusion about the *If*-side of the top layer. For example, look again at the rule tested above:

Rule

E   IF symptom swelling of   THEN there is evidence that
     the spleen is found   bug-eyed germs are present (.7).

Since the initial data didn't confirm Rule E directly, Unmycin is seeking an indirect confirmation, so it resurveys its knowledge rules, to find all the rules whose *Then*-sides state a conclusion about the data just requested, that is, about swelling of the spleen. Notice that the symptom swelling of the spleen was on the *If*-side in Rule E, whereas in the next three rules below it is on the *Then*-side.

Rule

E3   IF tight abdomen is ob-   THEN there is evidence for swell-
     served   ing of the spleen (.6).

E4   IF acid saliva preliminary   THEN there is evidence for swell-
     test is positive   ing of the spleen (.5).

E5   IF bad bellyache condi-   THEN there is evidence for swell-
     tion is observed   ing of the spleen (.3).

Unmycin wants to see if the data supports the *If*-side of rules E3, E4, and E5, so it asks the doctor questions for each of these, and the doctor types in the answers:

Data requested for:	*Unmycin asks:*	*Doctor types in:*
E3	Did you observe tight abdomen?	Present
E4	What is outcome of test for acid saliva?	Positive
E5	Is condition bad bellyache found?	No

Thus Rules E3 and E4 are confirmed. Thus *tight abdomen* (Rule E3) and *acid saliva* (Rule E4) suggest *swelling of the spleen* (Rule E) which, taken together with *yellowish skin cast* (Rule D), provides evidence for bug-eyed germs being the cause of the dreaded lurgy.

7. Computing the Certainty Factor. But just how good is the evidence for bug-eyed germs? Given the matches Unmycin found and the certainty factors stated with each rule, Mycin computes the likelihood that the presence of bug-eyed germs is indeed confirmed. It combines the certainty factors of each of the confirmed rules in such a way that each factor adds slightly to the overall likelihood. Certainty factors are not added together because that would lead to certainties greater than one—which is impossible.

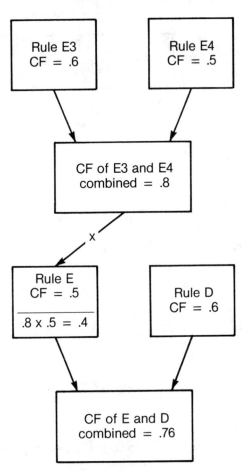

Observed disorder:

Goal selected to test for:

Level 1 rules that conclude
about bug-eyed germs:

Matched With clinical data:

Level 2 rules that conclude
about level 1 rule E:

Matched with clinical data:

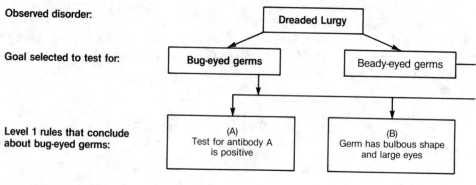

Figure 5–4
Unmycin's decision tree; using backward chaining to find cause
of dreaded lurgy

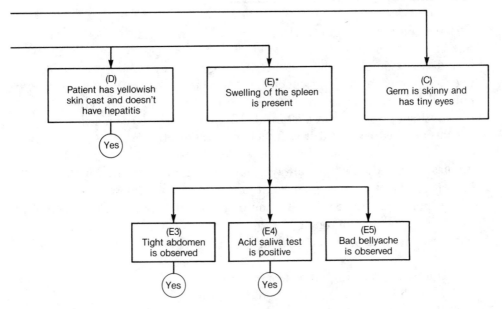

*Each of the other rules also has a branch of rules beneath it.
Only the rules invoked are shown here.

Calculating certainty factors in this manner is not statistically rigorous, but using the system over time has shown that it gives adequate answers. We should remember that the original source of the certainty factor for each rule is the gut feeling of the expert who helped develop the rule, and the certainty factors, like the rest of each rule, can be revised and corrected in light of experience with the expert system.

High Confidence From Low Confidence

We see that a doctor or Unmycin making a diagnosis gets around this inherent uncertainty by making a number of observations that are linked with some likelihood to a particular disease, and tying them together to reach a sound conclusion. If rules like these consistently pointed toward a particular disease, Unmycin wouldn't be needed. In the short run, neither the doctor nor Unmycin may be certain that the conclusion is correct. But it is sufficient to take action on.

This is the way any detective works. Outside the world of T.V. dramas, where the bad guy always confesses when confronted with the evidence, detectives and police and judges may never know for certain who committed the crime. "Beyond a reasonable doubt" is the criterion. So you look for enough rules to point convincingly toward a particular disease. Here's a final example:

If a patient has high blood pressure,
Then there is some evidence of heart disease.
If a patient has high cholesterol count,
Then there is some evidence of heart disease.
If a patient has some family history of heart disease,
Then there is some evidence of heart disease.
If a patient has chest pains,
Then there is significant evidence of heart disease.

None of these symptoms in itself points to an imminent heart attack, especially if the others are not found. But if all, or even most, of these symptoms are found in a patient, then the likelihood of heart problems is quite strong—but not absolutely certain.

CHAPTER 6

HOW THE COMPUTER READS KNOWLEDGE

- **Putting Uncertain Knowledge into Computer-Friendly Language**
- **How the Computer Computes With Knowledge**
- **Predicate Logic, Certainty Factors, Fuzzy Reasoning**
- **What Makes a Good AI Language?**
- **How Natural Is Natural Language?**

How can we express an expert's knowledge in a way that a computer can work with? From what we have said in previous chapters, this may seem like a paradox to you. On the one hand, we have contrasted an expert system to a conventional programming approach. We said that we cannot use a conventional programming approach for expert systems tasks because these tasks can't be reduced to a set of precise logical relationships and numerical formulas. But on the other hand, all computers deal only with precise, numerical relationships that can be reduced to "yes-no."

Perhaps we can portray this dilemma with the following dialogue between a programmer trying to program a computer to run an expert system, and the computer:

Programmer: Okay, Mr. Computer, here's what I want you to do. Take all this knowledge about how doctors diagnose diseases, use it to process these clinical observations and test results, and give me your best guess about what is wrong with this patient. There are many more rules than you need, so just select the ones you need, and ignore the rest.

Computer: Yes, Master. (Then it takes a microsecond or two to digest the input.) Hey, wait a minute, Nerd. What kind of stuff are you trying to push off on me. Look at this rule: The doctor says, and I quote: "There is some evidence that Test A means Infection B." Just how much evidence? I've gotta have precisely stated quantities, not all these maybe's and some-of-the-times. These rules are full of fuzzy concepts and ideas and loosely stated relationships. I've got to know precisely how things fit together, and what leads to what. Go back and reduce these to precise numerical relationships, and then bring them back to me.

And another thing. You've got to teach these people to speak my language. Here the guy says "inches" and over there "centimeters." Here a statement says "Enter the data," there it says "Input the data," and over here it says "Type in the data." I don't care what they say, but they must say the same thing the same way every time. No variation. It gives me a headache.

And look here! You say some of these rules may be changed later when you see how the first part works. I'm telling you, you'd better get all your rules down pat up front. Once I get my program set, it's a real problem changing it. Everything has to be just so, or I get totally confused. Great machine in the sky! Here you ask me to go ahead and reach the best conclusion I can, even though you might not have all the data I will need. How absurd. Have you looked at my job description lately?

So here is the seeming paradox. Expert systems are built from incomplete, imprecise, non-numerical knowledge, but they must run on computers, which operate using numbers—yes-no, on-off—and require complete programs. How does this paradox get resolved? How does this fuzzy, imprecise, uncertain, changing knowledge get put into "computer-friendly" language?

In this chapter, we will see what programming approach is required for expert systems tasks. This is a very large and complex subject, far beyond the scope of this book. And even if you were going to build an expert system using a program which is available today, you would be unlikely to get into programming at this level. But this question is too interesting to leave as a total "black box." So we will look briefly at the ways an expert's heuristic knowledge is expressed in computer friendly form, just to assuage your curiosity about what goes on at the deeper levels.

What Expert Systems Programs Require

To start, let's recap what we know about the requirements for building an expert system:

Characteristics for Expert Systems Tasks	*What Is Required*
An expert's heuristic knowledge is largely conceptual data and rules, which can't be reduced to a complete set of "yes-no" statements and numerical relationships. The rules are imprecise and the set of instructions will be incomplete.	The system requires great flexibility of expression. The developers must be able to express a great variety of concepts and functional relationships, which cannot be completely defined ahead of time.
The data on which decisions must be made will often be incomplete.	The system must be able to reach decisions with incomplete rules and uncertain data. It must be able to request additional data from the user even while the program is running.
The data and even the rules and instructions will change as the expert system is refined and upgraded.	The system must be easy to refine, even while it is being used.

The users are not computer experts, won't put up with a conventional computer language.

The expert system must understand the user's natural language statements and also "speak" in natural language.

The key to the programming approach is the programming language used. Let's focus on the features of AI languages that allow us to meet these requirements. The best known AI languages used to develop expert systems are Lisp and Prolog. We won't be concerned here with which of these is better. Lisp is used for most of the current expert systems, and Prolog is favored by the Japanese "fifth generation" AI computer programs, as reported in the *Fifth Generation Challenge* by Edward Feigenbaum.

WHAT MAKES LISP A GOOD EXPERT SYSTEMS LANGUAGE?

Let's look at the operation of our Unmycin expert system from Chapter 5. Expert systems like this one are often programmed in Lisp.

INITIAL DATA ENTERED BY DOCTOR		IF-SIDES OF RULES WHICH CONCLUDE ABOUT BUG-EYED GERMS		
Patient's age: 38	A	IF		Test for Antibody A is positive
Sex: M				
Medical history:	B	IF		Germ has shape: Bulbous
—			AND	Germ has character: large eyes
—				
—				
Results of lab tests:	D	IF		Patient has symptom: yellowish skin cast
—				
—			AND	Patient doesn't have hepatitis
Observed symptoms:				
Yellowish skin cast				
—				
—				

The first thing that we can explain using this example is the meaning of Lisp. Lisp means "list processor," and this means that Lisp works by processing items on lists that are linked in some way. In this Unmycin operation, Lisp is comparing the items on one list—the *If*-sides of certain rules—with items on another lisp—the clinical data about the patient entered by the doctor, to see if it can find a match. As we saw in Chapter 5, if a match was found the program did one thing, and if a match was not found, it did something else. This example highlights several key features of Lisp.

Turing test #2

Lisp Compares Apples and Oranges

Notice that in this example we were comparing two very different types of information: the list of data typed in by the doctor with a list of some of the built-in knowledge rules. Most programs can't do this. In conventional programming, the data that the user enters is structured very differently from the rules or instructions coded into the computer program, and these two are kept strictly separated. Data and rules are treated very differently, like apples and oranges. But one of the basic features of Lisp is that everything in the program—even the basic instructions—is treated as an element or item of data on a list. The knowledge rules and the data entered by the user are treated the same way, so we can easily compare apples and oranges. Treating all parts of the program as data on a list leads to several other key features of Lisp which allow an expert's knowledge to be expressed.

Lisp Allows Easy Revisions

As we saw in Chapter 4, when an expert system is being created, the knowledge engineer and experts don't know at first where the system will end up. They proceed by trial and error, there are many false starts, and the rules and even the basic instructions in the inference engine must often be changed many times. Often, they do not even know what size the final program will be. With Lisp, making revisions is simple. This is because Lisp treats everything—even the rules and instructions—as data, which can be easily removed or changed by the user.

In a conventional program, after the program is completed and tested, it is very easy to add or change the data. For example, if you have a spreadsheet program, you can easily change the numbers you use in a particular financial statement. But if you decide to change one of the underlying rules in this program about how financial data will be calculated, changing just one line of program instructions may require you to reprogram many other parts of the spreadsheet program.

Since Lisp treats all parts of the program as items of data on a list, you can easily revise or remove them as easily as you can change the financial data in a spreadsheet. This greatly simplifies revisions in the program—even the basic instructions contained in the inference engine rules.

Making Rules About Rules

Since rules and data are treated the same, an item can be treated as a rule at one time, then looked at as if it were data at another time. We can do such things as make rules about rules, which is essential for working out the most efficient heuristic search strategies.

Recall our automobile troubleshooter program in Chapter 5. There were rules which stated if such and such happens, then "check for loose battery wires," and if so and so happens, then "check for loose spark plug wires." When building an expert system it is essential to make the search through the rules as efficient as possible. So it is important to be able to go back after the program first runs and build in ways to make it run more efficiently. In this case, you would like to say to it, "If you are going to check loose wires for one thing, check for any other loose wires at the same time." After all, that is the way a busy human mechanic would do it. You would need to insert a rule about a rule, for example:

If   you check for any loose wire under the hood to satisfy any rule,

Then   examine all other rules which check for loose wires under the hood.

Subsequently, when this new rule is invoked, it will treat other rules as data no different from external data about whether or not the horn works.

A good expert system language must have a lot of flexibility for the user to enter a variety of heuristic rules of thumb at any stage as the program is being developed and refined. And since all items are treated by the Lisp program as data, they can be changed as easily as changing the financial data on a spreadsheet.

Another Lisp feature that aids efficient heuristic search is that the data entered at a particular point can control what the program does next. In the Unmycin example, when a piece of data is needed to answer a question posed by the expert system, the data fed in by the user determines the subsequent path of the search through the rules. A "yes" answer guides it down one path, a "no" answer down another, and a "don't know" down yet another. In computer parlance this is called "data driven programming." Most programs must follow a set sequence of rules, and do not have the flexibility to skip over to another branch of the decision tree when a particular response is received.

An Expert System Requests Input During Session

Lisp allows the expert system users to interact with it as it is running, or even earlier as it is being developed. With most programs, the user puts in all the data up front, making sure every piece of data is complete and precise. He starts the program running on the computer, and it runs all the way through until it reaches its answer. If the user has left out some piece of data, the computer just stops without completing the program. The user must locate the cause of the stoppage, insert the missing data, and start the whole program over from the beginning.

Lisp can deal with incomplete or missing data in several ways. First, as we saw in the Unmycin example, it can pause when it finds that data needed to reach a conclusion about an infection is missing and request it from the user by flashing a question on the screen. The expert system goes on "pause" while awaiting the user's response. The user can enter the data right then, or keep the system on hold while he conducts tests to get the needed data. When the data is entered, the system will continue from that spot and won't have to be restarted. Having your expert system program be interactive is a key feature, because you often don't know everything that you will need to know when you begin the session.

Reaching Conclusions With Uncertain or Incomplete Data

As we saw in Chapter 5, an expert system can proceed even when data is missing, and when the relationships stated in the knowledge rules are uncertain. The way it does this is the same way that a human expert does it. We do not rely on one line of inquiry, but look for a number of pieces of data which, taken together, allow us to reach a sound conclusion. As we saw in Chapter 5, if the expert system can't reach a conclusion by working down one chain of rules, it will go back to the top of the decision tree and start working down another branch of the tree.

Of course, if your expert system works through all the rules in its decision tree and just cannot find enough supporting data, it will inform its user: "I don't have enough data to reach a sound conclusion." A conventional program would not tell you this, it just wouldn't run.

The interactive nature of Lisp greatly aids the development of the expert system in the first place. In Chapter 4, we saw the knowledge engineer stop the prototype expert system program when the domain expert felt that one of its conclusions was inadequate and refine a couple of rules on the spot. Certainly an expert system can be programmed without these interactive features, but both the developers and the users would likely get very impatient, and would eventually get fed up and stop using the system.

How Lisp Allows Backward Chaining

We showed how Lisp allows one Lisp instruction to regard another instruction as a concept or piece of data to manipulate. A Lisp instruction can even regard itself as a piece of data, and can call on itself to help reach a conclusion. This bedrock feature of Lisp is called *recursion*, and allows Lisp to be used for many tasks which are very difficult in other programming languages. Recursion makes possible backward chaining, which is an essential search strategy for many expert systems.

The example that is always used to explain recursion is finding the factorial of a number. If you remember from algebra, the factorial of a number is that number times all the numbers below it, down to one. The factorial of 5 (which is signified by 5 followed by an exclamation mark) is

$$5! = 5 \times 4 \times 3 \times 2 \times 1$$

The factorial of 6 is:

$$6! = 6 \times 5 \times 4 \times 3 \times 2 \times 1$$

You quickly see that the factorial of 6 equals 6 times the factorial of 5, and $5! = 5 \times 4!$ and so on down to one. Seeing this allows us to state a general formula for calculating the factorial of any number. The factorial of any number n equals n times the factorial of $n - 1$. The equation is:

$$n! = n(n - 1)!, \text{ with } 1! = 1.$$

To find the factorial of n, you must calculate the factorial of n – 1, and to find the factorial of n – 1, you must calculate the factorial of n – 2, and so on. This seems complicated until you try to devise any other general formula for finding a factorial which you could plug into a computer. This formula is called *recursive* because it calls on itself repeatedly to solve itself.

Recursion underlies backward chaining. Look back at our Unmycin example, which started by seeking data that would indicate the presence of bug-eyed germs. Unmycin might state its strategy this way:

"Seek data that confirm rules that conclude about bug-eyed germs."

If it does not find the confirming data immediately, then it backs down the chain of rules one link and says,

"Seek data that confirm rules (on Level 2) that confirm rules (on Level 1) that conclude about bug-eyed germs."

And if it does not find data at that stage, it backs down yet another link and says,

"Seek data that confirm rules (on Level 3) that confirm rules (on Level 2) that confirm rules (on Level 1) that conclude about bug-eyed germs."

Unmycin can back down the chain recursively one link at a time by repeatedly calling on one basic instruction until it finds the confirming data or reaches the bottom of the chain, at which time it goes back to the top and starts down another chain.

Up to now, we have considered some of the features which allow your expert system to conduct efficient heuristic searches through the rules and to be easily refined. In the next section, we will see how an expert system can have an unlimited variety of concepts and relationships and instructions, and how these are built up.

HOW CONCEPTUAL RELATIONSHIPS ARE EXPRESSED

Expert systems are full of statements and instructions like these:

Compare the results of these tests with the If-Side of those rules, and see if there are any matches.

Find a space in a cabinet just large enough to insert Power Unit #2, and make sure it is no more than 30 inches from Cabinet B.

If rock formation Type A is present, and core test B suggests that rock Type B is not present, then increase the likelihood that Ore C will be found to 40 percent.

If the patient is allergic to any of the agents shown on this list, then do not prescribe penicillin.

Statements like these cannot be completely reduced to numerical terms; if they could, we wouldn't need expert systems.

What are the qualities of an AI language such as Lisp that allow a knowledge engineer to state any number of conceptual relationships and instructions to the computer? Lisp and other AI languages are based on *predicate logic* that is more complex and more flexible than the *propositional logic*, which underlies conventional programming and computers themselves. Let's see what the difference is and what difference it makes for expert systems. We will start by contrasting propositional and predicate logic.

Propositional Logic vs. Predicate Logic

Predicate logic is actually an offshoot of propositional logic, which in turn is the cornerstone of conventional computer programs, and in fact is the cornerstone of the computer's internal logic as well. Propositional logic is the logic of your sophomore philosophy class. Remember:

All Greeks are mortal
Plato is a Greek
Therefore, Plato is mortal.

Propositional logic measures the truth or falsehood of entire statements, or propositions, such as "Plato is mortal." These statements are compared and evaluated using a small number of logical operators:

Symbol	Pronounced	Meaning
$\land$ $\cap$	and	both
$\lor$ $\cup$	or	either or both
$\sim$ $\lnot$	not	the opposite
$\supset$ $\rightarrow$	implies	if the preceding term is true, so is the following term
$\equiv$	equivalent	has the same truth value

From these relationships are built up all the mathematical operators that both we and computers calculate with:

$$+, -, \times, \%, >, <, =$$

Propositional logic works fine for conventional programming statements, in which all the elements are true or false, or for discrete numbers or formulas. But suppose we have another statement, "Socrates is a Greek," and we want to use these same propositions to compare Socrates and Plato. Such a comparison would require making discriminations not just between propositions, but within a proposition, and this pushes the limits of propositional logic. Even statements such as "All Greeks are mortal" or "Find an example of a mortal Greek" are beyond propositional logic. Yet expert systems are built up from just such conclusions.

So propositional logic forms the foundation of conventional programming, but it has proven inadequate for representing the heuristic knowledge of AI programs and expert systems. For that we need predicate logic.

Predicate Logic Underlies Heuristic Search

Predicate logic allows us to evaluate individual terms within a logical statement or proposition. To see how predicate logic works, dissect one of those building blocks of expert systems—an If-Then rule—and label its parts.

If   the infectious agent is bug-eyed germs
Then   the patient's infection is dreaded lurgy.

First let's look at the second half of this statement, first in English, and beneath that, as it might look in Lisp programming code.

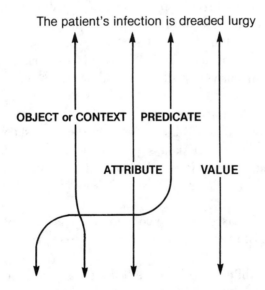

The patient's infection is dreaded lurgy

OBJECT or CONTEXT | PREDICATE

ATTRIBUTE | VALUE

Same context infection dreaded lurgy—lisp code

Predicate Functions. The predicate is the action word or the instruction in an If-Then statement. In that sense it is related to the grammatical predicate from freshman English, which is the verb, or action word, of the sentence. The logical predicate states the relationship which is being evaluated in the entire proposition. The entire If-Then statement contains two predicate functions: "if" and "then," which in Lisp could be rendered as "same" and "conclude."

Object. The overall "context" of the investigation, in this case the patient.

Attribute. That particular aspect of the object that this statement is checking. The patient has other attributes dealt with in other statements, such as age and any other possible diseases.

Value. The value of the attribute to be validated or rejected. The value is linked to the attribute by the predicate.

This entire statement is a logical proposition which is being tested by seeking confirming data, to see if the attribute "infection" and value "dreaded lurgy" linked by the predicate "is" is valid or not.

Suppose the data does not support the proposition, i.e., suppose bug-eyed germs are not found. Then the proposition will not prove true. But in Lisp, the opposite of "true" is not "false"—it is "nil," which means "no answer available," and which prompts the expert system to look further.

To sum up, the purpose is to determine the correct value of the particular attribute of the object. The predicate tests what type of relationship to test for. If data supports the premise that bug-eyed germs are present, then the *conclusion* "Patient's infection *is* dreaded lurgy" is *true*. Here's the crux:

Predicates are used to state conceptual relationships.
Objects, attributes, and values are used to express concepts.

There's a crucial difference: The predicate speaks to the computer and must be carefully defined in computer-readable terms. The objects, attributes, and values, on the other hand, are just linked symbolic concepts, which do not have to be understood by the computer, because it treats them merely as closed packets shoved around by the predicate's instructions. The computer behaves like a baggage handler in an airport who is told, "Go over to that baggage carousel and find the green suitcase that matches this one, if there is one, and bring it back here." The handler doesn't care what's in the suitcase. He just follows the instructions to match the packets. He looks only at the labels, not at the contents.

Thus any concept or statement can be stated using Lisp's predicate logic so that it can be manipulated by the computer. The ideas, the terms, the jargon of the expert can easily be included. But the relationships, as expressed by the predicates, are the critical factors.

Predicates Speak to the Computer

The predicates contain the information that the computer must understand and act upon. We have just seen two predicates—"same" and "conclude"—which are perhaps the most common in expert systems. And there are many other predicate functions used in expert systems which are defined in the code of Lisp or another AI language, including these:

Predicate Function	Meaning
APPEND	Add an item to the end of a list
SETQ	Assign a value to a variable
DEFUN	Define a function
GETPROP	Find a property of an object
PUTPROP	Add a property to an object
NULL	See if there are any items on a list
QUOTE	Don't regard this as a function; don't evaluate it
ISA	Is an example of

Each predicate function is defined in terms of other more primitive functions. At the base, Lisp is composed of a handful of primitive functions which on the one hand speak directly to the computer, and on the other hand, are ideal building blocks to express an unlimited variety of other relationships. Here are some of Lisp's primitive functions:

CAR	Retrieve the first element on a list
CDR ("Coudr")	Retrieve entire list except first element
CONS	Add a new first element to a list

The predicate functions that knowledge engineers use are quite far removed from these primitive functions. It is like comparing a finished carburetor, ready to use in a car, with machine screws, rubber gaskets, and sheet metal. But each predicate is built up step by step from other functions. For example, here is how the function APPEND can be defined:

```
(DE APPEND (L1 L2)
   (COND ((NULL L1) L2)
         ((ATOM L1) (CONS L1 L2))
         (TRUE (CONS (CAR L1) (APPEND
          (CDR L1) L2)))))
```

Defining New Predicates

With this capability to create and manipulate complex functions, a knowledge engineer can create a new function by combining existing ones. So virtually any conceptual relationship that can be stated logically can be expressed as a predicate function in Lisp. There are two very important consequences of this.

First, we can refine existing functions to make ever-finer distinctions. For example, if we had a predicate function SEE, and another one SHORT-TIME-DURATION, we could combine them and define the new function as GLIMPSE. Second, we can specify synonyms for functions. If our system has a function FIND, and some user is always asking it to "locate" a piece of data, we could just set LOCATE to be equivalent to FIND. FIND would not be replaced by LOCATE, as it would with many programming languages; but both functions would be stored on a list as equivalent terms. These features are key to the development of a natural language interface, as we will discuss later.

Having said all this, it is important to qualify our assertions. Not just any statement can be linked to the computer in this way. It must be structured in a particular way, and all the words must obviously be well-defined and always used in the same way. But If-Then rules do have a consistent format which is easily translatable to Lisp statements.

Down to the Hardware

If all this were not mind-boggling enough, Figure 6-1 illustrates the steps between primitive Lisp functions and the actual hardware of the computer. If complexity of the reasoning apparatus is any measure of intelligence, then we must be getting close to true artificial intelligence.

In summary, Lisp is the intermediary between the natural language of the expert and the computer's internal machine language. Predicate logic is a feature of Lisp. Lisp is constructed so that, on the one hand, complete English sentences can be expressed with their verbs, nouns, and modifiers. On the other hand, it is constructed so that the computer's logic circuits can directly interpret all its statements. Each of the Lisp predicates gives specific instructions to the computer, just like arithmetic operators $+$, $-$, $\times$, or $=$ do. So the relationships defined by all these predicates can be expressed in the yes/no language of the computer. Lisp allows any concept to be stated so that the computer can manipulate it. And predicate logic provides a set of verbs or instructions which express any kind of relationship the expert can state in a rule. So there are many constraints, but knowledge can be expressed.

HOW EXPERT SYSTEMS DEAL WITH UNCERTAINTY

Fuzzy logic allows an expert system to reason with uncertain data. Let's look again at how uncertainty arises in expert systems.

1. The heuristic knowledge rules which express relationships have uncertainty built into them. In rules like these below, the experts assigned only a certain likelihood that a particular observation indicates a given outcome.

If (1) The patient is shivering uncontrollably
   (2) The tests for minrovelli are positive
   (3) Blood serum levels are elevated
then there is suggestive evidence (level 0.65) that the patient
is infected with guy-fawkes virus

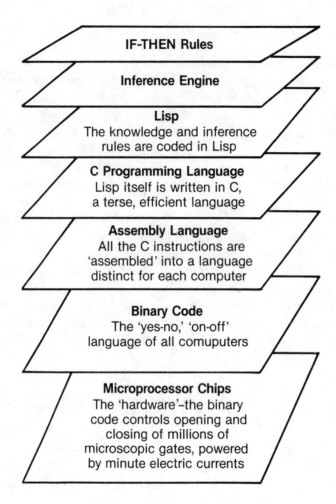

Figure 6–1
From expert's knowledge to computer language

The corresponding statements in LISP are:

PREMISE: ($AND (SAME CNTXT SHIVER UNCON)
                (SAME CNTXT MONROV POS)
                (SAME CNTXT SERUM ELEV)
ACTION: (CONCLUDE CNTXT IDENT GUYFAWKES
TALLY 0.65)

2. The data that the user of the expert system enters may not be certain. Clinical test results may be preliminary, and geological field observations may be misleading.

3. When these two sources of uncertainty are present, then the conclusions reached by the expert system are stated with a degree of uncertainty. In Chapter 5, we saw how certainty factors in the expert system's conclusion are computed from the certainty factors stated in the knowledge rules. (There is a real danger of confusion since the term "certainty factor" is used in two different ways here, and both of them really measure your uncertainty.)

Here is how certainty factors are calculated in an expert system like Mycin.

HOW A CERTAINTY FACTOR IS CALCULATED

The CFs of Rules E3 and E4 are combined using this formula:

The CF of E3 and E4 combined equals
the CF of E3 plus
the CF of E4 times (**1 minus the CF of E3**)

Or in shorthand:

$$CF (E3, E4) = CF(E3) + CF(E4) * (1 - CF(E3))$$

Inserting the numbers:

$$
\begin{aligned}
CF(E3, E4) &= .6 + .5 (1 - .6) \\
&= .6 + .5 * .4 \\
&= .6 + .2 \\
&= .8
\end{aligned}
$$

If we just added the certainties of E3 and E4, their combined certainty would be greater than 1. We modify the amount of certainty added by the second certainty factor by multiplying it by 1—the first factor. Thus the greater the first CF, the less certainty is added by the second. But additional factors will always add some confidence.

This is an example of how an AI language like Lisp can combine numerical computation with manipulating symbols and concepts.

Fuzzy Sets Allow Expert Systems to Handle Uncertainty

In addition to certainty factors, there is another method for handling uncertainty—called *fuzzy sets*—that is coming into use with some expert systems.. Let's see what fuzzy sets are, why they are important, and then see how they are used in an expert system.

Suppose we want to establish a chain of retail stores for tall men, and we need to find out what is considered to be tall. We can conduct a survey and ask people some things like, "How tall is a tall man?" or more precisely, "Where is the cutoff between tall and not tall?" Of course the kind of answer we would like to get from this survey is that every man over six feet is considered tall, and anyone shorter is not, as shown here.

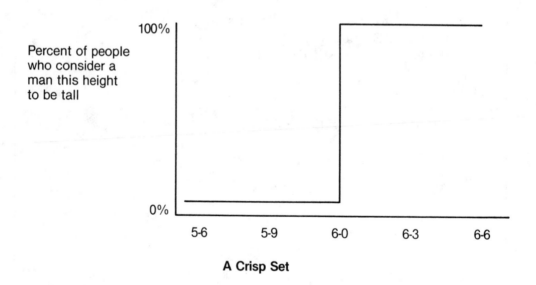

A Crisp Set

But opinions will not fall that way, will they? We will find that some people think 5-10 is tall, and some others think 6-2 is not so tall. Most everyone would agree that 6-6 is tall and 5-6 is short for a man. But in between, we would find a scatter of opinions like this:

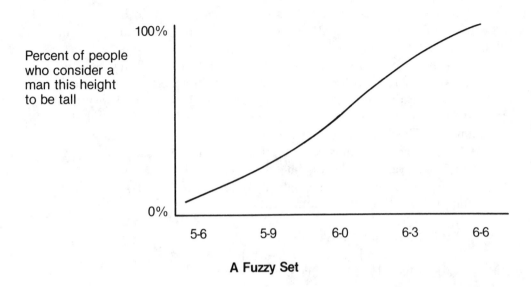

A Fuzzy Set

This means that for any particular height between 5-6 and 6-6, we can't say with certainty whether a man will be considered tall or not. In logic terminology, we would say that the set "tall men" does not have a clear or crisp boundary. It is a fuzzy set. For any height, there is a particular likelihood that a man will belong to the set "considered to be a tall man."

How are fuzzy sets used in expert systems? This notion can be applied to making a judgment about whether a person is sick or not, or whether a rock formation contains a commercial ore deposit. Suppose a patient has blood pressure of 84. Is this high blood pressure or is it normal? Does this indicate he has a high risk of heart disease? Some clinics select some cutoff point—say 86—and say everyone with blood pressure lower than that is safe, and anyone with a higher reading has high blood pressure. Yet a certain proportion of men with lower blood pressures do have heart disease, and some with higher pressures are perfectly healthy. Why don't we just move the cutoff point lower, so that we catch more sick people? This would increase the cost of screening and lead to unnecessary treatment of healthy people. Any arbitrary cutoff point like this will exclude some who should be included and vice versa. It would be more accurate to devise a fuzzy set to show how high the risk is that a man with a given blood pressure will develop heart disease.

If someone tells us that we are 60 percent likely to be sick, we would probably respond, "Well, am I sick or not?" We want a yes or no answer. One fuzzy set by itself is of little value. You cannot use it to draw a useful conclusion. Fuzzy sets are used in expert systems the same way certainty factors are. A fuzzy set is attached to each knowledge rule, expressing the likelihood that any particular observation made by the user will indicate a particular conclusion that is being evaluated. Then the fuzzy sets with each rule are combined to narrow the zone of fuzziness. For example, if we were using these in an expert system that evaluates the likelihood of heart disease, we would have fuzzy sets or certainty factors attached to a number of rules which would evaluate the data for a patient:

> Patient has cholesterol count of 95.
> Patient has family history of heart disease.
> Patient has blood pressure of 200 over 86.
> Patient is 48 years old.
> Patient is 22 pounds overweight for his height and build.

Each of these numbers falls at some point along the fuzzy set curve for that rule. Since none of them are at an extreme value, none of them by themselves indicate a high risk of heart disease.

Fuzzy sets are not fuzzy mathematics. Using mathematical formulas, the computer combines the values on each of these "broad" fuzzy values to obtain a final value on a "narrow" fuzzy value. The doctor could state the risk for heart disease with a much narrower zone of uncertainty.

As with certainty factors, fuzzy sets allow expert systems to combine several indicators with low levels of confidence to come out with one measure having a high level of confidence.

Fuzzy logic is another tool expert systems use to stimulate the way human experts think. Experts often do not initially assign things rigidly to one category or another. They say, "It might be here or it might be there." They do not settle which category it is actually in until quite late in the process, if they ever know. In fact, many of the things they consider might be changing even as they work on the problem. If a doctor is working on a sick patient, the disease state does not stay the same. The patient may get sicker or healthier while they are being studied.

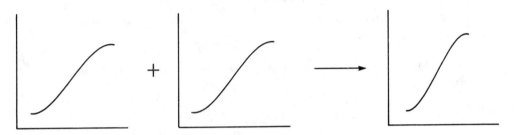

Two broad fuzzy sets combine into one narrow fuzzy set

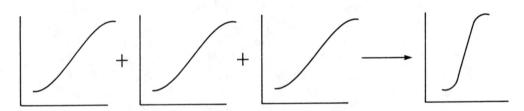

Three fuzzy sets combine into one that is even narrower

Some things are inherently unknowable until after a decision is made. Suppose geologists are using an expert system like Prospector to decide where to mine for ore. The field observations and core samples cannot tell them with certainty whether commercial amounts of ore are under the surface. They won't know until they dig. They would make a number of different observations, find where each observed value falls on the fuzzy set curve associated with that observation, and combine all the measures to get a value with a high enough confidence that they can make a reliable decision.

Certainty Factors vs. Fuzzy Sets

Fuzzy sets seem a little more complicated than certainty factors. Why not just use certainty factors all the time? Certainty factors are more appropriate for knowledge rules about two-value observations, like "yes or no" or "present or not present."

> *If*   test results are positive
> *Then*   there is evidence that patient has the dreaded lurgy.
>   (CF = .7)

Fuzzy sets are better for evaluating a numerical value on a spectrum of possible values.

> *If*   core sample shows tar particle concentration of 5%
> *Then*   there is evidence for commercial tar sands. (60%)

Fuzzy logic has not been used much in expert systems in the past because it is more complex to develop, and takes more computing power. But fuzzy sets are being used more in emerging expert systems.

Many expert systems don't use certainty factors to measure the uncertainty of a conclusion. They just reach yes or no decisions—is this the answer or not?—without worrying about probability. This depends on their task. For example, Dendral, which identifies the structure of chemicals, just reaches a single solution: "This is the one!" Once identified, there is no doubt about the structure. Likewise, R1, which lays out computer systems for large installations, will come up with one design that meets all the criteria programmed into it. The technicians check it to make sure it is correct. But R1 doesn't say, "I am 85 percent confident this is a workable design." There can be many workable designs for any particular system layout, but R1's users need only one design which is good enough.

NATURAL LANGUAGE ALLOWS COMPUTER NON-EXPERTS EASE OF USE

"I can tell from your voice harmonics, Dave, that you're badly upset. Why don't you take a stress pill and get some rest?"

HAL, the 9000 series computer, in *2001: A Space Odyssey*

When you hear the term "natural language" used regarding computers, you may get an image of someone having a conversation like this one with HAL. It has been a longtime dream of AI experts to develop a program which can carry on a general conversation like this.

This, however, does not reflect reality. First of all, we can't talk with computers yet. A few prototype computer systems can recognize a handful of spoken commands from a known voice in quiet surroundings. Computers are quickly learning how to *create* spoken responses, as anyone knows who has called Directory Assistance for a phone number lately. Even a computer's ability to understand sentences typed in on their keyboard is severely limited, although expanding rapidly. And that is what we will discuss here.

Many expert systems interact with their users in natural language. As you saw in previous chapters, instructions and questions appear on the computer screen in English sentences, and the user types responses and instructions in English sentences, words, or phrases. This natural language capability is very important for expert systems, because the professionals who use these systems just would not be bothered to use them if they first had to learn the terse commands of standard programming languages.

This is even true for the people developing expert systems. We have portrayed the specialized knowledge engineer, the skilled Lisp programmer, and the domain experts putting their heads together to transmute knowledge into computer code. But as expert systems proliferate, less skilled programmers will be responsible for entering knowledge rules and organizing and revising the rule base. A natural language interface will allow them to enter If-Then rules in this form:

If (1) The patient is shivering uncontrollably
   (2) The tests for minrovelli are positive
   (3) Blood serum levels are elevated
then there is suggestive evidence (level 0.65) that the patient
is infected with guy-fawkes virus

rather than in this Lisp form:

```
PREMISE: ($AND (SAME CNTXT SHIVER UNCON)
               (SAME CNTXT MONROV POS)
               (SAME CNTXT SERUM ELEV)
    ACTION: (CONCLUDE CNTXT IDENT GUYFAWKES
    TALLY 0.65)
```

For the most part, as you have seen in this book, when we speak of computers which communicate with their users in natural language, we mean that they use highly-structured sentences which all have very similar formats, with no wasted words. Every term must have a specific, well-defined meaning.

Nevertheless, this limitation is less important than it might appear when expert systems are involved. If you listen in on the conversation in a chemistry lab or operating room while two doctors are focusing on a tough problem, their talk sounds just like that. You hear short, clipped sentences, full of technical terms, whether requests, statements, or questions. So for these environments, the computer's language really is natural.

Natural language does use English words (or French or Japanese or whatever). So the term contrasts with most common programming languages, such as Fortran or Pascal, which are designed to make programming efficient, but cannot be read by non-programmers.

In the mid-70s, when Mycin and others were first used, their natural language capability was novel. However, this distinction will be increasingly blurred as more and more common software programs adopt a natural language interface for the user. Anyone who wants to can get such programs as word processors, databases, or spreadsheets which you can program or instruct using everyday words, often selected from a menu on the screen. And this is certainly true of the emerging expert system development programs. But the distinction is still very important in a couple of areas, as we will see below.

The natural language interchange between an expert system and its user or developer is a two-way interchange. The computer makes statements and asks questions, and the user enters data and rules and other statements and also asks questions. So we must discuss both aspects: the ability of the computer to speak in natural language, its ability to understand the natural language statements made by the user. It is much easier for the computer to "speak" natural language to the user than to understand the user's natural language input. Let's show a few examples of each, and you will see why this is true. Remember, every time we say "speak" we mean that words appear on the computer screen, either from the computer's innards, or typed in by the user.

The Computer "Speaks" in Natural Language

We have seen above, the computer speaks in several different situations: It asks the user questions, states its conclusions, and explains the reasoning behind its conclusions. When the computer is ready to communicate its conclusions or questions or explanations to the user, it doesn't create new sentences from a general vocabulary. Instead, it has a built-in "canned" response for each rule and situation it must respond to. Let's look at two examples from our Unmycin session above. First, recall when a rule couldn't be matched with the needed data, and the expert system had to request more data from the user. There is a special instruction which takes a piece of the rule, and inserts it into a template for a question. Illustration 6–6 shows the rule with the missing data highlighted. Figuratively speaking, this piece is pulled out and inserted into the template for requesting data.

Likewise, the expert system states its conclusions to the user by taking pieces of the rule it has just confirmed, calculating the certainty factor as shown above, and sticking these into a "conclusion template," like this:

Unmycin: I conclude that the patient has dreaded lurgy caused by bug-eyed germs with a certainty factor of .76.

CONCLUSION TEMPLATE	PIECES OF RULES INSERTED
I conclude that <object of evaluation>	patient
<template words adjusted for proper tense>	does have
<attribute>	dreaded lurgy
caused by	
<confirmed value of attribute>	bug-eyed germs
with confidence of	
<calculated value>	76

Expert systems that can provide explanations for reaching conclusions or for requesting data use a similar process. This is a bit more difficult, because the computer might have to recall an entire sequence of rules it has used to reach a conclusion. However, expert systems hold in their active memory all these rules it has used, just for this purpose. (If only we humans could so easily explain why we do what we do!) Suppose Unmycin had been asked why it concluded that the patient had dreaded lurgy. It would recall this sequence of rules, and construct the explanation below, using a stored "explanation sentence fragment."

Doctor: WHY? (Since this question followed a stated conclusion, Unmycin interprets it to mean, "Why did you conclude that patient's dreaded lurgy was caused by bug-eyed germs?")

Unmycin: I concluded that the patient's dreaded lurgy was caused by bug-eyed germs because tight abdomen (E3) and acid saliva (E4) indicate swelling of the spleen (E), which taken together with yellowish skin cast (D) provide evidence (CF = .76) that bug-eyed germs are the cause of dreaded lurgy.

Here's how Unmycin's response was constructed by inserting pieces of the rules it used into a template.

CONCLUSION EXPLANATION TEMPLATE	PIECES OF RULES INSERTED
I concluded that	
<restatement of the question>	the patient's dreaded lurgy was caused by bug-eyed germs
because	
<second level rules confirmed by data>	tight abdomen acid saliva
<first level rules confirmed by second level rules>	swelling of the spleen

<first level rules confirmed by   yellowish skin cast
data>

provide evidence for

<the confirmed hypothesis>   dreaded lurgy
                                     caused by bug-eyed germs

<calculated confidence factor>   (CF = .76)

As you see from this example, there is more to it than just tapping into
the right response and flashing it on the screen. The expert system's
natural language program has rules built into it which examine the
sentences before they are flashed on the screen to make sure they read
correctly. It adds in articles—a, an, and the—as needed, and keeps the
verb tenses and the noun numbers consistent. For example, it knows
when to use "is" and "are" and when and how to change the singular to
the plural.

How the Computer Understands What We Say

Natural language understanding by computers is in its infancy. It
is a much more difficult process for the computer than translating its
internal workings into a structured sentence. However, rapid strides
are being made in this field, for upcoming expert systems, and for
other devices.

Let's be clear about what we mean by natural language understanding. The computer must understand you when you say things in
your normal way. In contrast, with any other system, you must learn
to say things the way the computer can understand them. This may
mean using the terse terms of a programming language, or using a
limited set of English words in a specific order. The crucial difference
is, who teaches whom? Does the computer learn to understand how
you say things, or must you learn how the computer understands
things? With true natural language understanding, the computer can
understand anything you could type in that another person could
understand. Today's best natural language systems do not meet that

standard: They are partway between this point and a programming language.

Many, but not all, expert systems must be able to understand whole sentences typed in by the user. The expert systems which incorporate natural language programs are the ones which would not be useful if the users could not pose unpredictable and unstructured statements and questions. For example, the users of Mycin must request many explanations of its conclusions, and they must be able to ask questions like these:

Is blood a sterile site?
What are the nonsterile sites?
What organisms are likely to be found in the throat?
Are bacteroides aerobic?
What methods of collecting sputum cultures do you consider?
What dosage of streptomycin do you generally recommend?
How do you decide that an organism might be streptococcus?
Why do you ask whether the patient has a fever of unknown origin?
What drugs would you consider to treat e. coli?
How do you use the site of the culture to decide an organism's identity?

WHY IS NATURAL LANGUAGE SO DIFFICULT FOR A COMPUTER?

English is full of ambiguities. Consider these sentences:

The doctor saw the germs in the blood sample with the microscope.
The doctor saw the germs in the blood sample with the low white cell count.
The doctor saw the germs in the blood sample with apprehension.

Or these, in which one idea can be expressed in many ways:

Tell me why you reached that conclusion.
Can you tell me how you reached that conclusion?
What are your reasons for making that decision?
I would like to see all the rules you applied to conclude that.

Or this one which demonstrates that many statements can be read in several ways, which can be determined only from the context:
"They are flying planes."

They are (flying airplanes).
They (are flying) airplanes.
They are (flying planing tools).
They (are flying) (planing tools).

Next consider condensed meanings, like this sequence of questions:

What is the patient's prognosis?
What are his greatest risk factors?
His areas of no risk?

Finally, our sentences are full of misspellings, and are often ungrammatical and incomplete.

Whats the patents blod count.

How does the expert system understand sentences like these? Let's look at two ways—one which seeks to avoid most of these problems, and another which tackles them head on.

Menu-Driven Natural Language

The natural language interface of some simple expert systems is menu driven. This means that for any situation the user encounters, he can select words needed to build up a sentence from a sequence of menus which he can make appear on the computer screen, as on the illustration below. The highlighted words are those selected to construct a sentence.

FUNCTION	New Rule	Explanation Template		Query
patient disease organisms blood test	is are has does have indicate use conclude	what is which what how do you know how did you use how how many	rule organism patient blood test site threat	with about of for from in

QUERY SO FAR: What organisms are in throat?

If you have used a computer which uses a mouse to select items from the computer screen, you know how fast this can be done with a little practice. The benefits of this approach are readily apparent: It circumvents many of the ambiguities of the English language by having the user select words and word orders that the computer already knows. But the drawback is equally apparent: The user can say nothing new that isn't already in the computer. This approach works very well for some tasks, but many expert system tasks cannot be defined well enough, or the terminology is not consistent enough, for this approach to be adequate. The interesting and innovative questions cannot be restricted by having a menu-driven interface. It is for precisely those tasks for which expert systems are most needed that the ability of the user to state new things in a variety of ways is most important.

Understanding Any Structured Sentence

At the other end of the spectrum of approaches to natural language understanding is the *syntactic grammar program* which breaks down any sentence entered into elements that it can analyze for meaning.

Let's look at the process the computer uses to understand this sentence:

What organisms are likely to be found in the throat?

First, it breaks the sentence down by a process called "parsing." Do you remember that term from freshman English? In English class, parsing is the process of breaking a sentence down into nouns, verbs, prepositional phrases, and so forth. The computer parses a sentence in a similar way. Here's how it would parse this sentence.

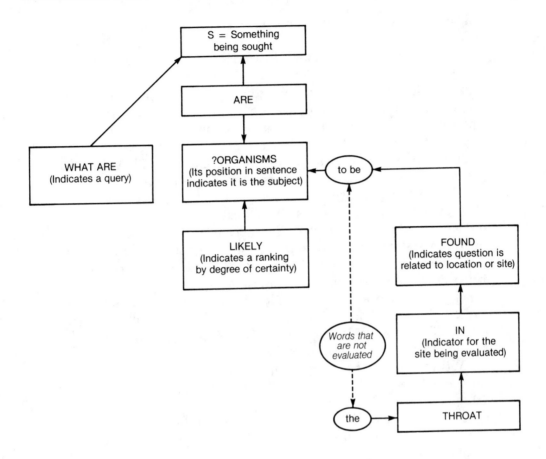

Figure 6–2
Parsing a sentence into understandable pieces

In this way it recognizes and classifies verbs, nouns, modifiers, objects, subjects, and "noise words" like articles. Words are recognized using several strategies. First it strips away the words it recognizes as nonessential for the sentence's meaning. The remaining words are reduced to root words. It seeks the meanings of these key words in their root form using its internal dictionary, which defines words by relating them to other words. In many cases, when a word can have more than one meaning, it classifies words by where they are in the sentence, and in relation to other key words. Some terms are translated to numbers: "weak evidence, some evidence, suggestive evidence," become .2, .4, .6, etc.

Next it analyzes the pattern of words in the sentence, to decide what kind of sentence it is. Is it a question, requesting information, or an explanation? Or a statement, inputting data? Finally it identifies the key words, which will trigger its response. In a medical diagnostic expert system, this could be the patient's name, the infection being considered, a rule in the system, or something else the system is familiar with and knows how to respond to. Once it understands the question or instruction, it constructs its response in the way we outlined in the section above.

How good is this approach? The vocabulary, the sentence structure and word order are limited. Yet there is some flexibility. It gives the expert system the ability to understand instructions and responses to questions in varied format. It can learn to understand synonyms or shades of meanings, as long as the user defines them in terms that are already in the vocabulary. These additions are made in the same way that new Lisp functions are defined; in fact, it is essentially the same process. That is why Lisp or a similar language is so often used as the basis for a natural language interface.

We may never have full natural language understanding on a computer. There will always be a tradeoff when it comes to expert systems. Even if it were technically reachable, it would be very expensive to develop. And expert systems developers and users don't need a chatterbox able to converse about anything and everything. On the other hand . . .

So for the time being, we have reached a middle ground. A certain amount of flexibility is built in, but it is still rather constricted. As we said above, it doesn't matter too much. Expert systems are used for tasks in narrowly defined problem areas. The people who work on these problems are professionals who have a specialized jargon. When they are on the job, they often speak to one another using short structured statements loaded with precisely defined terms. So the freedom of expression they have with the natural language interface of an expert system is adequate for their needs.

As expert systems become more widespread with people who are not highly trained professionals, the natural language capability will have to become more generalized. The limitations to the system's language capability, besides our ability to program into a computer all the vagaries of the English language, are the memory and speed of the computer. Due to the complexity of everyday language, these are crucial limitations for even the largest computers, and even more so for expert systems that will run on a microcomputer. But as memory capacity and processing speed rapidly increase, before long desktop computers will be powerful enough to contain a thorough natural language understanding capability.

THE DRAWBACKS OF AI LANGUAGES

All the power and flexibility of languages like Lisp have a cost. First, we got an inkling that this flexibility is achieved through complex and often convoluted programming code. Lisp is difficult to program, and top-notch Lisp programmers are rare and expensive. Second, more programming code means more computer processing time. These programs take longer to run and require larger computer memories to hold the larger program all at one time. For example, here are comparative times required for several languages to complete the same task—the redesign of a 24-transistor cell:

OPS5, an AI language related to the one from which R1 was programmed, with an interactive version of Lisp, took 8 hours of computer time.

Lisp version with reduced ability to be interactive took 45 minutes.

Prolog, the second most well-known AI language, took 10 minutes. Shorter time was at the cost of less control over the redesign process.

C, a very efficient programming language, took 1 minute.

So why not stick with C? If any changes are needed in the redesign process, the C program would require substantial overhaul, whereas the expert systems versions would require only the change of a few rules.

Third, AI languages are not needed for straight computation. They can perform calculations, but, again, not as efficiently as can the more terse conventional programming languages. For example, consider 2 plus 2:

In BASIC programming: X = 2 + 2

In Lisp   (SETQ X ADD (2 2))

For large, complex calculations, Lisp becomes very cumbersome.

Expert Systems Are Often Reprogrammed

Because Lisp or Prolog run slower than conventional programming languages, expert systems are often reprogrammed into another language when the knowledge engineer is confident that few if any changes remain to be made. This is particularly true for the inference engine rules. These instructions which embody the basic problem-solving strategy get solidified long before the knowledge rules do. For many expert system tasks the knowledge rules will always be changing, but the inference engine gets stabilized. This is one of the chief reasons why the knowledge base is separated from the inference engine. At that time, the inference engine rules are rewritten into a programming language like C or Basic or Pascal. Thereafter, the expert system can run much more rapidly.

THE BENEFITS OF AI LANGUAGES

Let's recap the ways that an AI language such as Lisp allows a computer to understand and work with an expert's knowledge. Complex instructions and relationships contained in knowledge rules can be expressed using predicate logic. The experts assign certainty factors to all their "maybe's" and "most of the times." Using these, the expert system computes a confidence level for its conclusions. Some expert systems use fuzzy sets to express data which is by nature uncertain. Natural language interfaces can be built which allow users to ask questions or enter data or rules in the way they speak, rather than in a formal programming language. The expert systems are able to pause and request needed data, and to explain the reasoning behind their conclusions.

Summary

Our purpose in this chapter has been to shed a little light on the mysterious process of how an expert's knowledge—conceptual, fuzzy, idiosyncratic as it is—can be molded into a form the computer's silicon chips can use. We have barely scratched the surface. There are many different ways to do all this, and we have shown just a couple of representative examples. If you wish to find out more about this, check the books recommended in the reading list at the end of the book. But if this has been quite enough to boggle your mind, let's go have a beer.

CHAPTER 7

DEVELOPING YOUR EXPERT SYSTEM

- Early Expert System Shells and Their Descendants
- Unzipping One Knowledge Base and Adding Another
- Expert Systems Development Tools
- The Quality of Your Expertise Is Still Crucial

Suppose we wanted to build our own expert system. Would we have to go through this painstaking knowledge engineering process we have been discussing? Not at all. Our way has been smoothed. There are now software programs we can buy to guide us in developing our own expert systems. Equally important, many of the newer systems can run on smaller computers. In this chapter, we will discuss some of the programs for developing expert systems, and see what tasks they are good for. We will also see how these packages evolved from the pioneer expert systems.

Stripping Knowledge from the Expert System

In Chapter 4, when we discussed the knowledge engineering process, we noted how important it is to keep the knowledge base separate from the inference engine. This allows us to change the knowledge rules and expand the capabilities of an expert system easily as our knowledge and needs change. Developers of expert systems quickly discovered that they could remove all the knowledge rules from a system, leaving only the inference rules and the natural language interface, insert a new set of knowledge rules, and—lo and behold—create a brand-new expert system for an entirely different task.

How can we remove the knowledge rules from an expert system and retain the inference engine? Remember that the inference engine is the part of the expert system that holds the instructions for searching through the knowledge rules to find a solution. In Chapter 5, we discussed different heuristic search strategies. The inference engine for any expert system is built around a particular search strategy appropriate for the system's task. We saw that different types of tasks require different search strategies. For some tasks we start with a proposed solution and work backwards to the evidence, and for others it is better to start with a set of facts and work forward to the best solution. On the other hand, some seemingly unrelated tasks can actually use the same search strategy. For example, diagnosing human diseases and troubleshooting balky TV sets may use very similar reasoning processes, whether done by a human expert or a computerized expert. Let's make this point more concrete with an example using a human expert. After all, knowledge-based expert systems are modeled on approaches successful human experts use to solve problems.

Our Transferable Problem-Solving Strategies

Suppose you are a hot-shot computer troubleshooter. You can diagnose any malfunction of any personal computer, and you have a couple of sure-fire approaches to identifying any malfunction.

One night as you sit hacking at your computer, your children come in and say their video cassette recorder (VCR) is broken. You reluctantly pull yourself away from your computer. You don't know anything about VCRs, but there you are standing in front of the dead VCR, with your children looking on expectantly. How do you troubleshoot this creature? Well, you say, troubleshooting is troubleshooting, so you put computers out of your mind for a moment, and focus on your skills in diagnosing malfunctions in electronic gadgets. What is the problem before you? What could have caused it? What problems can you quickly eliminate? You ask all the same questions that guide you while troubleshooting anything. You quickly discover that your children know everything about the VCR's operation; they are like a knowledge base and database—whatever you need to know, you ask them. You take the role of the inference engine, and together you make up an expert system. So you identify possible problems and ask them questions to help you confirm or reject each possibility. What they don't know, you figure out by reading the VCR manual. Before long you have found the problem and have *Raiders of the Lost Ark* running again for the 147th time.

Human experts are good at applying their general problem-solving expertise in one area to another area. Once we learn how to perform one task, it is usually much easier to learn how to do a second, related task. Of course we must somehow master all the needed facts and knowledge about the unfamiliar problem area, but our skill at solving problems transfers from one area to another.

Expert System Strategies Are Also Transferable

Expert systems have this same capability, to a limited extent, and this is one of their most important features. Among the first to discover this were the developers of Mycin at Stanford University. They recognized that the same approach Mycin uses to diagnose infectious blood diseases is applicable to diagnosing a variety of other disorders. An expert system needs new knowledge about the new disease, but its knowledge about how to *diagnose* a disease by matching rules to evidence is still valid. Remember that the expert system's problem-solving strategy is built into its inference engine as a set of inference rules that tell the system how to search through its knowledge rules. And just as with human experts, the strategy for searching through rules is to some degree independent of the problem to be solved.

Let's see how Mycin and some other early expert systems were used to develop additional systems, and then look at a few of the recent expert systems derived from them. We will see that these new, derived systems are easier to use and require smaller computers than their parent systems did. We will also get a better idea of the kinds of tasks each family of expert systems is appropriate for.

THE MYCIN FAMILY—FINDING CAUSES AND PRESCRIBING CURES

Mycin provides a good example of how a new expert system can be created from an existing inference engine. Remember that the Mycin program consists of these parts:

1. **A knowledge base of 500 rules about how to spot infectious diseases from fragmentary evidence, and what drugs to prescribe for them.**
2. **An inference engine—the rules that tell Mycin how to apply the knowledge rules to find a solution.**
3. **A natural language interface, which tells Mycin how to ask questions in English, interpret users' answers, explain its conclusions, and so on.**

This is diagrammed in Figure 7–1.

MYCIN

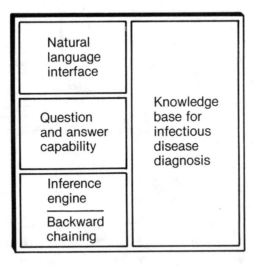

Figure 7–1
Mycin's structure

When Mycin's knowledge base for infectious disease diagnosis is removed, the inference engine and the natural language interface are left, as illustrated in Figure 7–2. The part of Mycin remaining is referred to as Essential Mycin, or Emycin.

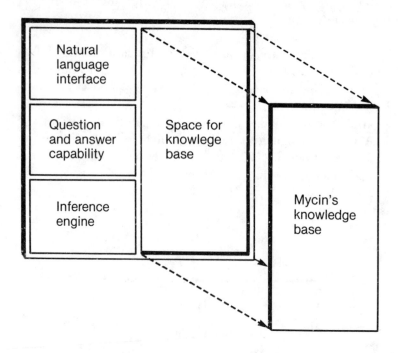

Figure 7–2
Mycin's knowledge base is removed, leaving Emycin

The Emycin Expert System Shell

By attaching new sets of knowledge rules to Emycin, two new expert systems—Puff and Oncocin—were created. To create Puff (short for Pulmonary Function disorder diagnosis) a set of knowledge rules was developed to diagnose breathing disorders. These rules were crafted into a knowledge base structured just like the knowledge base of infectious disease rules in Mycin. This new knowledge base was then inserted into the Emycin shell (Mycin's inference engine), where the Mycin rules had been, and a brand-new expert system was born. Doctors in this field now had another knowledge-based diagnostic system to work with as well as Mycin.

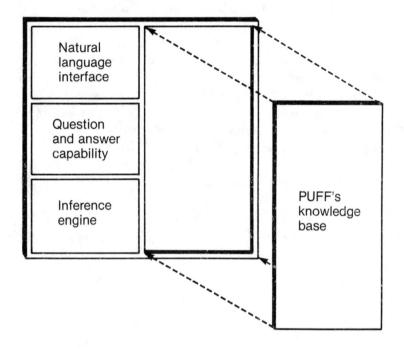

Figure 7–3
Inserting pulmonary disease knowledge base into Emycin to create PUFF

Emycin was also used to develop Oncocin, which is used to diagnose cancers. Again, a new rule base was developed by knowledge engineers and cancer experts and crafted to fit into the Emycin shell.

Sacon—A Non-Medical Offspring

If we can put in rules to diagnose other kinds of human disorders, why couldn't we use the same inference engine with new knowledge rules to diagnose other kinds of disorders, say computer malfunctions or automobile breakdowns? And this is exactly what has been done. Emycin has been applied to a number of different diagnostic situations, each with its unique knowledge base. But one of the earliest applications was called SACON, for Structural Analysis CONsultant. SACON advises nonexpert engineers to use a specialized computer program called MARC to perform structural analysis of objects, such as the possible metal fatigue in an airplane wing. MARC has tremendous capabilities to simulate many structural analysis situations and problems, but it is very complex to learn to use. Engineers know what they want to do, but have difficulty figuring out how to use MARC to do it. It takes a year of training to master its bewildering variety of options and constraints. SACON helps engineers translate what analysis they want to perform into a sequence of tasks for MARC.

Although its task seems very different, there are key similarities. To a computer, looking through a set of rules to find a match with observed symptoms looks very similar to looking through a set of options to find the combination that best meets a desired outcome stated by the engineer and recommending the appropriate action to take.

Teiresias—the Guide to Building Rules

To make Emycin easier to use, another piece of the program was developed, called Teiresias, for the purpose of guiding the knowledge engineer in the creation of rules for a new expert system built for the Emycin shell. Teiresias is actually a separate expert system, designed for the task of building or revising other expert systems.

While Emycin is designed to start from scratch building a new knowledge base, it was not designed to help the knowledge engineer test and debug the new knowledge rules interactively. Teiresias does this.

Teiresias itself is programmed in Interlisp—a version of Lisp with many interactive features added—but it is designed to interact with its users in natural language. Teiresias works by greatly expanding the explanation facility we briefly described in Chapter 6. If the user finds that a set of knowledge rules leads to an inadequate conclusion, he can have Teiresias show on the computer screen all the rules used to

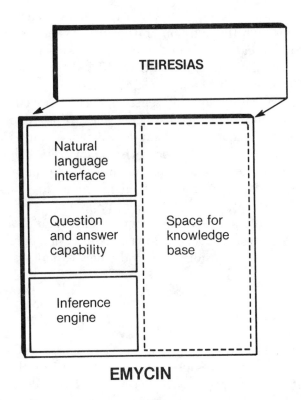

Figure 7–4
TEIRESIAS added to Emycin to guide rule creation and editing

reach that conclusion. Using the rule editor, adjustments in the rules can be made on the spot, and the program can be immediately rerun to show the impact of the rule changes. When a new rule is entered, Teiresias tests its understanding by translating it from natural language into Lisp, and then retranslating it to natural language. It also politely points out to the user inconsistencies and inadequacies it spots in the rule base.

Teiresias' features have been merged with Emycin, and have been used to create other expert systems such as Oncocin.

KS300—the Expert System Development Program

Emycin was still basically an experimental and demonstration system, even with the addition of Teiresias. When its developers left Stanford and created Teknowledge, they restructured Emycin and made it more efficient. The result was KS300, an expert system shell designed for developing commercial systems.

The most significant difference between Emycin/Teiresias and KS300 is the addition of what has been called a "programming environment" which is a more visual way for someone who is not a professional programmer to enter or revise knowledge rules. This is an essential step in the commercialization process of expert systems. With the addition of the programming environment to the shell, KS300 became an expert system development program.

KS300 is still an expensive system, which requires a special computer designed to run Lisp programs. Its price included a knowledge engineer to help the customer build the new expert system.

Drilling Advisor

One successful expert system developed using KS300 is Drilling Advisor, which was developed by Schlumberger, the large oil drilling firm. Getting drill bits stuck in bore holes deep beneath the surface is a major problem for them, and to get the bits loose often requires a thorough knowledge of the kind of rocks it is stuck in. A few experts have long experience interpreting the instrument readings from these bore holes and recommending the best strategy for freeing the stuck bits. But these experts are scarce and expensive. So putting their knowledge onto an expert system seemed a cost-effective alternative.

Drilling Advisor contains about 300 heuristic rules plus descriptions of about 50 drilling parameters. Drilling Advisor is used by the drilling supervisor, who can work with it in either English or French. Its inference engine starts with the most likely problems and reasons backwards, seeking supporting evidence from instruments in the bore hole. Once the most likely problem is pinpointed, the best action to free the drill bit is suggested.

M.1 and S.1: Expert System Development Programs for Microcomputers

M.1 and S.1 represent the next stage in the further evolution of Expert System Development Programs toward ease of programming and use on smaller computers. To make KS300 even more commercially available, its programming environment and inference engine were again rewritten and made more compact, so that it would run on a smaller computer such as an IBM PC. The resulting product is called M.1. To squeeze M.1 into the capacity of a PC, certain compromises in its power and capabilities had to be made and these limited its commercial acceptability. Perhaps too much had been removed. So M.1 was again souped up and S.1 was created (which requires a supermicrocomputer to run on). Internally, they both contain inferencing rules very similar to Mycin's. But the user never has to see these rules.

M.1 and S.1 are designed to make the process of building expert systems even easier. As you can see in Figure 7-5, they contain a knowledge engineering interface which helps you create knowledge rules, review and edit your rules, enter data into its database, and review its reasoning by viewing the path it takes through its decision rules. All this is done without any knowledge of a computer programming language.

Expert System Development Programs

So we have traced the evolution of expert system development programs from Emycin to the most recent packages (some key systems are illustrated in Figure 7-6). The evolution has been in two directions: first, toward programs requiring smaller computers, and second, toward easier means of developing and programming the knowledge rules. Evolution in both these directions continues.

Expert systems developed from Emycin perform many different tasks. Yet as varied as their tasks are, the systems are all based on the same approach: All identify a problem, diagnose the cause of the problem, select the best solution among a limited number of possible

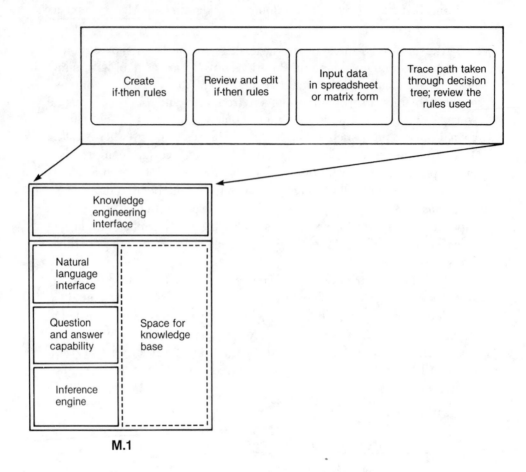

Figure 7–5
M.1's knowledge engineering interface

solutions, then prescribe appropriate action. Since they are all developed from Mycin, each of these systems uses the backward reasoning approach we described in Chapter 5. This factor is both a strength and a limitation. It limits the applicability of the system to tasks that can be formulated as making a selection. Backward chaining on a small computer is impractical when there are too many possible solutions, as we saw with R1 or Dendral, because not enough alternate solutions or knowledge rules can be held in memory.

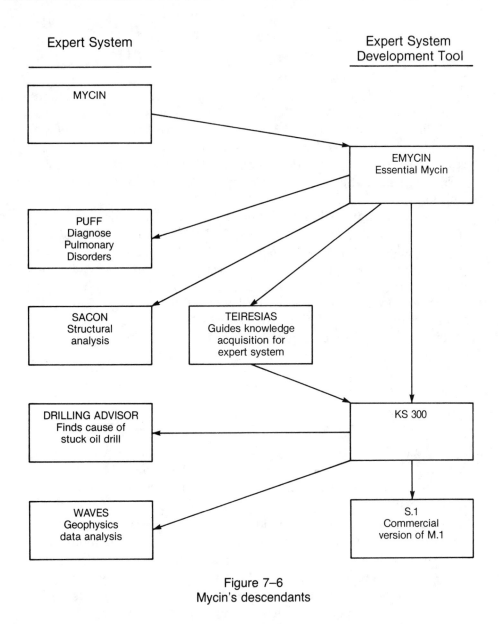

Figure 7–6
Mycin's descendants

Speaking of R1, let's now see the similar evolution from a couple of other early expert systems to current expert system development tools.

THE R1 FAMILY—DESIGNING LAYOUTS AND SCHEDULES

Another early expert system that has spawned expert system development tools is R1, or XCON. R1, as we saw in Chapter 2, has a very different task than does Mycin and thus works in a completely different way. R1, used by DEC to help configure VAX systems, must lay out a variety of computer components and connectors, given a variety of constraints and special requirements, so that they all work well together.

As with Mycin, R1's earliest spin-offs were created for tasks quite similar to its own. R1 or XCON led to XSEL and XSITE, two systems that were designed to ease further the task of designing and laying out VAX computer systems. They were basically extensions of XCON. R1 was created using a programming language called OPS. Due partly to the experience with R1 and its offshoots, OPS has been continually refined into a tool for building expert systems. The latest version—OPS5—runs on a microcomputer.

Airplan

The next system made from the R1 mold, Airplan, was developed for a task that at first glance appears very different from R1's. Airplan is used to schedule flight training for aircraft on aircraft carriers. Its job is arranging and rearranging time slots to make the best use of aircraft for training. There are many different types of aircraft, each with its own requirements for support team, landing and take-off, preparation, storage and maintenance, and so on. Some aircraft can be used together, some must be used separately. And the schedules are always changing due to weather conditions and other factors. Airplan looks at these time and resource needs for each aircraft in just the same way that R1 looks at the components and connections for a complex computer system. From a computer's point of view, selecting computer components that fit together is very similar to selecting time slots that fit together.

The Hearsay II Family—Recognizing Patterns

Hearsay II is an expert system designed to recognize speech. It can recognize sentences spoken within a certain narrow range of sentence structures, and can understand about 1000 words. The words must be used in a context with distinct, pre-defined meanings.

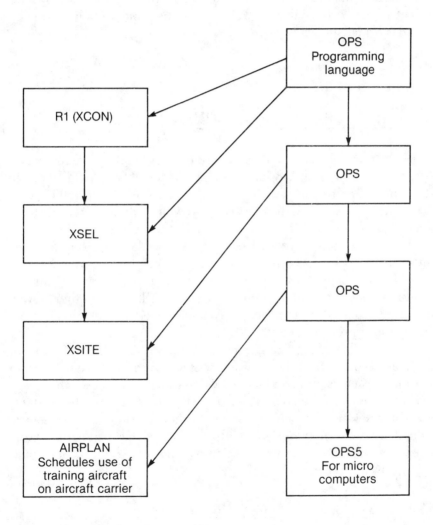

Figure 7–7
R1's family

Hearsay is composed of several separate parts, or modules, each of which is a complete expert system in itself. A separate part analyzes and understands nine different aspects of spoken speech, such as word meanings, word order, sentence structure, etc. Each level supplies data on what it deduces about its part to a central "blackboard" within the computer. The overall controlling program then selects data from each source which it deems relevant to interpreting the speech fragment it is currently analyzing. It does all this rapidly enough to keep up with normal speech.

Hearsay II's ESDPs—Hearsay III and AGE

Even though Hearsay II is experimental, it has spawned several descendants. You could say that Hearsay III and AGE (for Attempt to GEneralize) are related to Hearsay II as Emycin and KS300 are to Mycin. They have both been used to develop other expert systems which share characteristics with the task of speech recognition.

HASP and SIAP are two expert systems developed from AGE which are used by the Navy to interpret sonar signals from submarines. The problem they face is picking out recognizable, recurrent patterns among the jumble of noise the sonar picks up. Another system developed from AGE is called Acronym, which is used by the Air Force to interpret photo images.

You see that recognizing patterns from sensory data is the common feature of each of these systems. Each of these systems uses an instrument such as a microphone or video camera to receive the image or sound from the outside world, and then converts whatever it receives to a set of electronic signals that other instruments can analyze for patterns. These patterns are then matched against patterns the system contains in its memory. The user is alerted whenever meaningful patterns are recognized.

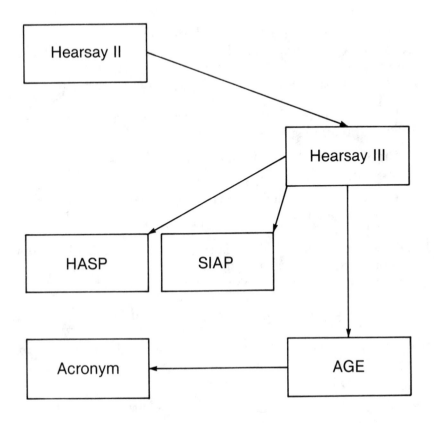

Figure 7–8
Hearsay II's family

These tools all require the knowledge engineer to enter rules in Lisp and even to determine just which strategy the inference engine should use, so they are not simple enough for commercial applications. Yet there is a very strong demand for computer-based systems that can recognize speech, visual images, and other such patterns, and these require the type of approaches used in Hearsay II and the ESDPs derived from it. Thus, much effort is being directed toward development of such systems. Despite the difficulties involved, we will likely see a variety of these systems during the next few years.

ESDP FAMILIES

We have sampled ESDPs derived from three early expert systems. Each family is structured quite differently and is useful for tackling diverse types of tasks requiring very different strategies. Here's how we might characterize the problem-solving approach of each family.

The Mycin family finds the best option among several possibilities, reasoning backwards.

The R1 family designs layouts and schedules, using forward reasoning.

The Hearsay II family recognizes meaningful patterns among a welter of input.

ESDPs that can handle other classes of problems have been developed from other early expert systems.

TABLE 7–1
Some of the early expert system shells

Name	Source ES	Applics	Common Chars	Year developed
OPS5	OPS	R1	Forward chaining	1977
EMYCIN	MYCIN	PUFF	Backward chain	1979
ROSIE	RITA	General purpose	Interactive	1981
KAS	PROSPECTOR	Selection	Forward and backward chaining	1981
EXPERT	CASNET	Ophthalmology endocrinology rheumatology		1979
HEARSAY III	HEARSAY II	Understanding complex signals	Multiple cooperating modules	1980
AGE	HEARSAY II	Design and testing	Multiple cooperating modules	1979

SELECTING THE BEST ESDP

The problem facing the potential expert system developer is figuring out beforehand how to characterize the problem to be solved so he or she knows which ESDP to buy. This requires looking at problems in unfamiliar ways. As we have seen from the examples presented in this chapter, many seemingly dissimilar tasks actually use the same problem-solving approach. Whether scheduling training flights is more like designing computer systems or diagnosing disease, for instance, may not be obvious. To select the best ESDP, you must learn to take a "computer's-eye view" of our tasks, and what is required to accomplish them successfully. One valuable by-product of this exercise is a new discipline in conceptualizing and classifying problems.

Wouldn't it be nice, though, to have an ESDP which is flexible enough to handle many kinds of problems and that includes a module to help us decide which problem-solving strategy our task requires? Let's look at a few ESDPs that are moving in this direction.

THE GAMUT OF AVAILABLE ESDPS

If we want to buy a software package to help us develop an expert system, we already have a broad range of tools to choose from. Just the ESDPs we have discussed so far are suited to a very broad spectrum of tasks, computer power, and financial resources. And, of course, new commercial programs are continually coming into the marketplace. "Commercial" means that they are packaged in ways which make it easier for people who aren't AI programming experts to define a suitable task for an expert system, and develop a knowledge base adequate for accomplishing this task. Many of them also run on smaller, more affordable computers.

Most of these new packages are not descended directly from the pioneer expert systems, but they are based on the same problem-solving strategies. With such a welter of options and competing claims, how do we choose the best package? Let's divide the ESDPs into four broad categories:

1. **ESDPs for microcomputers, based on a single inference strategy.**
2. **ESDPs for microcomputers and super microcomputers, with several inference strategies built in.**
3. **ESDPs designed for building expert systems in a specific field, such as financial services.**
4. **Turnkey expert systems developed from a particular ESDP, with a built-in knowledge base for a particular function, such as financial planning.**

These four categories do not fall along a spectrum, but instead represent the evolution of ESDPs in two directions: one toward more powerful and flexible systems, and another toward systems which are very easy to use but restricted to a specific task.

Microcomputer ESDPs

M.1, mentioned earlier in this chapter, and Expert-Ease, which we introduced in Chapter 3, are examples of ESDPs that run on an IBM PC or similar microcomputer. To both the developer and the user, these appear quite different from the early expert systems. Such systems include extra modules that overlay the internal inference rules, as shown in Figure 7–5. These modules, often called the "knowledge engineering toolkit," guide you through the process of building up, testing, and refining your knowledge rules. Depending on the complexity of the system, this toolkit might include the following:

> —**A worksheet format into which we insert examples of the facts from which our system's rules will be built. We saw in Chapter 3 how this works. We entered data from many instances into the worksheet, and Expert-Ease used a built-in program to develop rules, using induction. We didn't consciously create rules. This was done for us. The more examples we entered, the better our rules became.**

—A rule editor, which works like the editor part of a word processor. As we enter our rules in whatever form is called for, the editor allows us to review our rule base and change any rule. We can do this either as we are first programming, or later as we refine our system.

—A built-in library of case studies, so that when we change or add a rule, we can immediately test the revised system against the cases with known outcomes to see whether it reaches accurate conclusions.

—A template or set of guidelines for organizing the knowledge rules for the most effective searches.

—A graphic display of the path through the rules the system took to reach its conclusion. You can view the systems path through the decision tree, like the ones for backward and forward chaining displayed in Chapter 5.

Since these run on smaller computers, they cannot do as many tasks as the ESDPs for larger computers. They cannot handle as many rules or consider as many possible solutions. However, the memory capacity and processing speed of personal computers is growing rapidly, thus permitting systems with bases and many more rules to run on microcomputers. One feature of many such programs for microcomputers is that they are based on a single inference strategy. Many can do backward chaining but not forward chaining.

ESDPs with Multiple Search Strategies

Some of the ESDPs have a variety of problem-solving capabilities built into their inference engines. KEE (for Knowledge Engineering Environment) or ART, for example, allow users the option of forward or backward chaining, or of using both for different parts of a task.

For many tasks, multiple strategies are essential. Many problems don't fit neatly into one category, and different problem-solving strategies are needed for different parts of a single task. For example, suppose a task has too many possible solutions to fit neatly into backward chaining, yet lacks sufficient data to reach a single conclusion through forward chaining. You might want to use forward chaining to whittle down the number of plausible solutions to a manageable number, then use backward chaining to direct the search for the additional data needed to pinpoint the best solution.

Because these ESDPs combine different search techniques, they can be used for more kinds of problems. But there is a trade-off. The more flexible and powerful a package is, the more time and skill it takes to build a workable system from it. Greater capabilities require more powerful, more expensive computers, and more highly skilled people to program them correctly in the first place. The programs themselves cost much more as well.

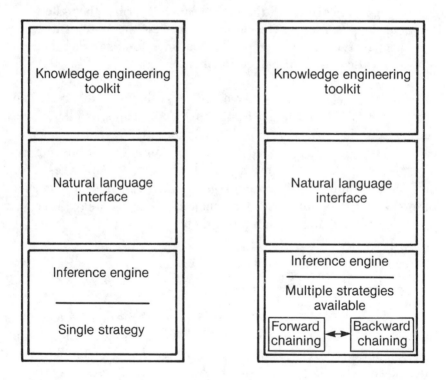

Figure 7–9
Single strategy ESDP (e.g., M.1, S.1) and multiple strategy
ESDP (e.g., KEE, ART)

ESDPs for Particular Applications

All of the systems discussed so far in this chapter are designed to be bought by large companies or institutions to develop their own expert systems, which they then use internally. But recently some companies have bought ESDPs, developed them partially or completely into expert systems for a particular application, and then resold them to companies that need just those systems. Reveal is an example of an ESDP designed for a particular type of application—bank finance and loan package analysis. The Loan Arranger system we used as an example in Chapter 1 was based on Reveal.

Turnkey Expert Systems

We will soon see complete expert systems, with knowledge bases already built into them, springing into the marketplace—expert systems to aid insurance underwriters, financial advisors, or loan officers. Sales Edge and Negotiation Edge from Human Edge Software, mentioned in Chapter 1, are early examples of these, and much more sophisticated programs will soon appear.

Initially these will be prepared for large companies that can afford the steep initial development costs. However, within a couple of years after proprietary models are introduced to large companies, we can expect similar versions to become more generally available. A company that wishes to produce a turnkey expert system may start from one of the ESDPs. As portrayed in Figure 7-10, the company would use the program's knowledge engineering aids to build and test their special knowledge base. Then the knowledge engineering part of the program would be removed before it was sold, because the end-user would not expect to make further changes in the system.

How Flexible Can They Get?

Each program or shell we have discussed was designed to handle a certain class of problems, and each has its strengths and weaknesses. With ESDPs getting more and more flexible, will we soon see one

Stage one

ESDP purchased or specially created

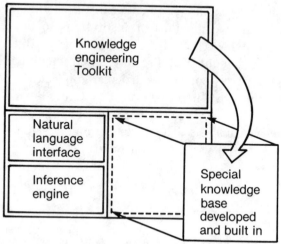

ESDP and knowledge base developed by software firm

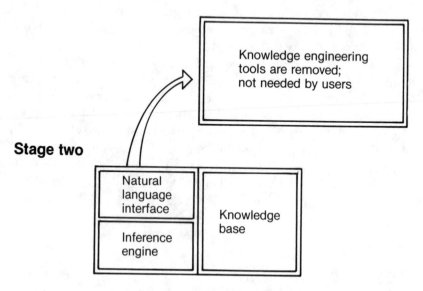

Stage two

Completed ready-to-use package sold to a vertical market

Figure 7–10
A turnkey expert system

that can be programmed to tackle any type of problem? Will we soon be able to buy general problem-solving frameworks? The answer is no. ESDPs are not at all general problem-solving frameworks. In fact, the artificial intelligence community would love to create such a framework, but it has never been successful in doing so. No computer program is as good a general problem-solver as any ten-year-old child.

THE QUALITY OF YOUR EXPERTISE IS STILL CRUCIAL: WATCH OUT FOR "GARBAGE IN, GOSPEL OUT"

The biggest difficulty and challenge with any of these systems is getting the knowledge into the system that will allow you to reach useful and valid conclusions. The biggest danger is mediocre output because of poor knowledge and decision rules. You don't have to learn Lisp or Prolog, but you still have to be a knowledge engineer to build a useful system with even the most "novice-friendly" package. As you build your system, you must keep in mind all the issues we discussed in Chapter 4 and go through all the same steps: identifying the problem, dividing the problem into pieces your system and your computer can handle, carving out the knowledge rules, and making your system run as efficiently as possible so that it will reach a reliable, valid conclusion.

Otherwise, your system will exhibit the malady of all mediocre computerized systems, "Garbage In, Garbage Out." You will also face the risk that information spewed from a computer under the guise of "expert advice" will be believed, even when it is mediocre; that is, "Garbage In, Gospel Out." Regardless of how large or how small the system is, quality of input and, hence, output is still the biggest challenge.

Selected ESDPs showing the variety of features, price, and size of computer required

TABLE 7–2

ESDP	DEVELOPED BY	WRITTEN IN	FEATURES	COMPUTER	PRICE
Emycin	Stanford Univ.	Interlisp	Backward chaining	Lisp machine	
KS300	Teknowledge	Lisp, based on Emycin	backward chaining	VAX Xerox	
M.1	Teknowledge	Prolog	backward chaining accesses a database	PC	$2000–10,000
S.1	Teknowledge	Lisp	backward chaining	VAX or Lisp machines	$50,000–80,000
Expert-Ease	Human Edge	UCSD Pascal	induction from examples	PC	$700
Exsys	Exsys, Inc.	C	induction from examples or create rules	PC	$295
ART (Advanced Reasoning Tool)	Inference Corp. (Los Angeles)	Lisp	backward and forward chaining; blackboards	VAX or Lisp machine	$85,000
KEE (Knowledge Engineering Environment)	Intellicorp (Menlo Park)	Lisp	BC, FC and Framp capal	Lisp machine; e.g., Symbolics	$60,000
Insight Knowledge System	Level 5 Research	Turbo Pascal	accesses a database	PC	$95
Personal Consultant	Texas Inst.	Lisp	based on Emycin	TI Personal computer	$4500– $25,000
TIMM (The Intelligent Machine Model)	General Research Corp. (Santa Barbara)	Fortran 77	induction from examples	PC	$9500

CHAPTER **8**

THE PROMISE OF EXPERT SYSTEMS

- **What Expert Systems Are Paying Off Now**
- **The Problems With Expert Systems**
- **Are Expert Systems Intelligent, Even Artificially?**
- **What's Coming, and What Impact Will It Have?**

To examine the promise of expert systems, we must first look at where the field is now, what the problems with expert systems are, and in what direction the development of expert systems seems to be going. This will help us evaluate the claims for and against expert systems and to decide whether we should develop our own system, and what would make it worthwhile for us to do so.

WHAT EXPERT SYSTEMS ARE PAYING OFF NOW

As we have seen in the preceding chapters, most of the early expert systems were developed primarily for research and demonstration. They didn't have to pay for themselves in the marketplace. The companies now developing expert systems are more demanding. Many AI research projects have been shelved because they didn't make economic sense, even though the system may have been technically feasible.

Nevertheless, many companies and institutions have recently developed successful expert systems—some from scratch and some using ESDPs like those we described in Chapters 3 and 7. Let's look at a few of these successful systems, and then ask: Given the current state of development of expert systems, when does the effort required to develop them pay off?

To evaluate where expert systems are now, we will look at a few expert systems that are currently being developed or used by large companies or by the government in situations where they must pay for themselves. We will briefly describe a few of those systems and then draw some lessons about what circumstances justify the investment of money and time required to get an expert system running at the current state of the art. In Chapter 2 we saw what technical considerations would justify developing an expert system. Here we will look at the economic justifications.

Boeing Prevents Valuable Knowledge from Retiring

Back in the mid-1970s, Boeing Aerospace Company realized that two of its most successful aircraft designs were nearing the end of their anticipated lifecycles and would soon have to be replaced with the next generation aircraft design. At the same time, Boeing saw that several of its top tool-design engineers were also approaching retirement age. Boeing was thus faced with the prospect of having to rely entirely on its younger generation of design engineers to develop its new aircraft designs.

How could Boeing's younger engineers gain the experience of the soon-to-retire senior engineers? Boeing first created design teams pairing a junior with a senior engineer and gave each team a computer-aided design (CAD) workstation. The teams had never used CAD systems before, but they jumped right in, and their productivity quickly shot up. But there was an unexpected second benefit. Just through the process of using the CAD systems for many different design projects, the memories of the CAD software were soon filled with visual design elements that captured the knowledge of the senior engineers, built up over an entire career, yet very difficult to convey deliberately to the younger engineers. By the time the older engineers

retired, not only had the junior engineers gained much of their expertise, but the company had the beginning of a permanent library of
design principles which could be continually built upon and used to
train new designers.

Using this expertise recorded by the CAD systems as a spring-
board, Boeing has gone on to pioneer a series of expert systems over
the last decade. Boeing's expert systems include a helicopter repair
advisor, a space station designer, and an airplane engine troubleshooter. It has worked in conjunction with Stanford, Carnegie-Mellon,
and other universities, and it has opened its own Artificial Intelligence
Center for research in expert systems and robotics and to train its own
people.

These are full-scale mainframe systems, and they were very expensive to develop. Why has Boeing felt this effort to be worthwhile?
The growth and profitability of the company depends on the excellence
and cost-effectiveness of its aircraft designs. Yet there are never enough
highly skilled engineers available to meet its needs. By capturing the
expertise of skilled engineers in an expert system, the next generation
of top engineers can be trained and the knowledge can be passed on.
Just as important, this also allows less-skilled people to tap into the top
expertise in the field.

NASA's Space Shuttle Reentry Navigator

As the space shuttle comes down out of orbit into the atmosphere,
it is constantly buffeted off course. Things happen very rapidly. It took
three navigators at mission control to operate the console that keeps
the shuttle on course. They monitored 100 instrument inputs and fifty
status lights and continuously made course adjustments calculated by
the computer to ensure the shuttle's safe descent. It took eighteen
months to train the few people who could deal with the complexity and
pressure of this task.

Now NASA has NAVEX, Navigation Expert System, to help bring
the shuttles down safely. One console operator using NAVEX does the
work of the three operators, and the performance of NAVEX is equal
or better than theirs. NAVEX monitors all the instruments and computes the course corrections. The operator in turn monitors NAVEX

and decides whether or not to implement its decisions. NAVEX works up to eight times as fast as the three-navigator team and avoids the human tendency to focus on one problem at a time. It greatly reduces the stress level of this job and drastically reduces the time it takes to train navigators.

NAVEX was developed using an expert system development tool called ART, Automated Reasoning Tool, from Inference Corporation in Los Angeles. A knowledge engineer from Inference, using ART and working with NASA's console operators, developed a NAVEX prototype in just five weeks. Then, because ART allows programmers without an extensive AI background to develop full-scale expert systems, NASA people were able to continue NAVEX development after just a week's training in ART. ART is written in Lisp and requires a large computer such as a Xerox 1108 or DEC 780 or a special Lisp machine. ART sells for $85,000.

NAVEX thus manages a crucial, complex, and stressful task, for which skilled people are very rare and expensive to train. It performs as well or better and can be operated by people who needn't have rare skills. If the space shuttle is ever to achieve commercial viability, such expert systems are essential.

Drilling Advisor

Drilling oil wells is a chancy and expensive operation at best, fraught with hazards. Getting the drill bit stuck in a bore hole thousands of feet beneath the surface is one of the most expensive problems. Oftentimes, the whole operation must shut down—at the cost of $100,000 per day—to wait for the arrival of one of the handful of experts worldwide who knows how to get the drills unstuck. It's an art, learned over years of experience, to interpret the instrument readings received from the point in the bore hole at which the bit is stuck and then to deduce the precise action to take to free the bit.

The art of the drilling expert was first reduced to a set of heuristic rules by Elf-Acquitaine, one of France's largest oil drilling firms. Using KEE from IntelliCorp, which we described in Chapter 7, they built an expert system called Drilling Advisor. Just as with Boeing's expert systems, Drilling Advisor has captured the knowledge of the rare senior expert and made it available to technicians with less experience. KEE is an expensive system, requires knowledge engineers and Lisp programmers, and takes a large computer. But with downtime costing $100,000 a day, this expert system doesn't take long to pay for itself.

Financial Advisors on a Disk

Many banks are busily developing expert systems that capture the experience of their top loan officers in sizing up loan applicants. These capture not just the formulas loan officers use to analyze the applicant's financial statements and the condition of the applicant's industry, but also all the subjective factors—the loan officer's "sixth sense"—which leads them to grant a loan to an applicant who looks questionable on paper, or to turn down an applicant who looks good. This allows junior loan officers to draw on the expertise of the most successful lenders as advisory systems.

Furthermore, loan officers must have at their fingertips an enormous amount of constantly changing data—on industry conditions, interest rates, tax law, credit ratings of the applicant's customers, and so on. Systems that make available the latest updated data and, coupled with the heuristic rules, are providing a service that easily pays for itself and provides better service to the clients.

In Chapter 1, we voiced the concern that lenders would put too much reliance on the dumb system and lose the human element. But from experience so far, the reality seems the opposite. Bankers who feel unsure of their ability to make good decisions tend to be too conservative and to turn down potentially good loans. This costs the bank just as much as granting poor loans. So these expert loan advisors allow more people to make better decisions. Banks keep their clients happy and improve their own profitability.

Other industries are developing similar systems. For example, large insurance companies are developing advisory systems to aid their underwriters in sizing up potential underwriting risks and to help evaluate the legitimacy of a claim. Organizations of financial advisors are refining systems to help members analyze their clients' financial situations and needs, and to recommend appropriate investment strategies.

When Does It Pay to Develop Expert Systems?

Are expert systems paying for themselves? It is still very expensive and time consuming to develop an expert system, even using the new expert system development programs. Thus the initial high hopes of many AI proponents have not yet been realized and many expensive projects have been quietly shelved. And yet an ever-growing number of companies and agencies are fielding expert systems and other AI products that are paying their own way.

The examples cited here show us that there are several good reasons to develop expert systems. Let's quickly review the factors that make a task a good candidate for use of an expert system. These criteria must be met in addition to the ones summarized on page 48, Common Characteristics of Expert System Tasks. That list focuses on factors which make an expert system technically preferable to a conventional programming approach. Here we summarize circumstances in which expert systems are worthwhile economically.

With NAVEX, and with R1 which we saw earlier, there are just too many factors for even the expert to handle. With Drilling Advisor, the expert isn't there when you need him, and the wait is very expensive. Boeing was prompted to build expert systems by retiring experts and the shortage of new experts that threatened to hold back the firm's development and profitability.

Expertise is often needed to augment the knowledge of junior personnel so that they can make better decisions. Examples include the advisory systems for bank loan officers and insurance underwriters. Some expert systems make one type of expertise available to people in a different field, so that they can make better decisions. Expert systems are used where there is rapid turnover in an organization, which is always having to provide costly and time-consuming training for its new people.

With NAVEX and with medical diagnostic systems, decisions must be made under a lot of pressure, and humans might forget a key factor. Or, as in the case with Dendral, there may be too many factors or possible solutions for a human to keep in mind at once, even when the problem is broken down into smaller pieces.

For some tasks, a huge amount of data must be sifted through to find the answer, as is the case, for example, with Prospector and its offshoots. For others, factors are constantly changing, and it is very hard for a person to keep on top of it all, and find what is needed at just the right time. In addition, there are several factors common to most problems that can be effectively handled by expert systems:

—The cost of a poor or delayed solution is very high.
—The problem *requires* a knowledge-based approach. It cannot be handled just as well by a standard computational approach.
—It is consistency, not creativity, that is essential.

A rapidly growing number of expert systems such as these pay their way, despite these rigorous criteria.

THE PROBLEMS AND THE PROMISE OF EXPERT SYSTEMS

A prominent factor common to all the expert systems described here is that they have all been developed by big organizations with lots of resources. Where is the flood of knowledge-based products for our home and office and school computers? What's holding it back? What must happen before the promise of expert systems is realized, if in fact it ever is? Let's look at some of the factors currently limiting the spread of expert systems, and how these are likely to change. Many of the problems holding expert systems back will likely be overcome within the next few years, so that in the near future, expert systems will be more accessible to all of us.

Why Do We Not Have Sherlock?

Remember Sherlock, the expert system sleuth we discussed in Chapter 1? This is certainly the kind of problem we would like to be able to program a computer to help us solve. Why doesn't such a system exist already? Answering this question will illustrate some of the difficulties faced by the developing expert system field, and will also show how quickly they could be overcome.

WHEN EXPERT SYSTEMS PAY FOR THEMSELVES

- The expert isn't always available. Retiring. The expert is very expensive or rare.

- A shortage of experts is holding back development and profitability.

- Expertise is needed to augment the knowledge of junior personnel.

- There are too many factors or possible solutions for a human to keep in mind at once, even when the problem is broken down into smaller pieces.

- Decisions must be made under pressure, and missing even a single factor could be disastrous.

- A huge amount of data must be sifted through.

- Factors are constantly changing, and it is very hard for a person to keep on top of them all and find what is needed at just the right time.

- One type of expertise must be made available to people in a different field so they can make better decisions.

- There is rapid turnover, a constant need to train new people. Training is costly and time consuming.

- The problem requires a knowledge-based approach and cannot be handled by a conventional computational approach.

- Consistency and reliability, not creativity, are paramount.

As we discuss the difficulties of building Sherlock, we will also compare Sherlock to Mycin to help gain perspective. The problems involved in creating Sherlock are much tougher than those involved in creating Mycin because Sherlock is much more complex. Sherlock's designers would have to combine expertise from several different fields; a nationwide network and database would have to be created; the amount of data required might tax the largest computers; and once Sherlock was operational, the system would require constant updating.

The Knowledge Isn't Readily Available

One obstacle to the development of Sherlock is that the models and profiles that Sherlock requires do not exist. Various experts and knowledge engineers would have to develop profiles of both runaways and kidnappers, and then link these to particular actions and patterns of behavior that could be observed and recorded. To develop these profiles, knowledge engineers would have to draw upon knowledge from detective work, criminal psychology, and child psychology, and even identifying all the factors that need to be considered would be difficult.

This would be a very tough—and very expensive—knowledge engineering task. The designers would have to get the experts together and work with them over a long period of time. Even so, it is unlikely that all these experts would agree on the profiles or on the best approaches to identify the people sought. All this varied information would also have to be reduced to some consistent format for the computer. Reconciling diverse and disagreeing sources of knowledge greatly complicates the task of engineering an expert system.

Contrast this with Mycin. Much more concrete information about Mycin's field is readily available. There are doctors who are acknowledged experts at diagnosing infectious diseases from observed symptoms and test results. Furthermore, a handful of diseases accounts for the vast majority of diagnoses made. Mycin, even with its 500 knowledge rules, has many fewer variables to consider than Sherlock. We are also much better working with things we can see and take samples of than with matters of the psyche. There currently is no expert system that diagnoses and prescribes treatment for mental disorders, and this is a likely starting place for developing the psychological profiles needed by Sherlock.

Testing Is Difficult

But suppose we were able to develop the needed behavior profiles. Once a prototype Sherlock system was available, it would require an extensive period of testing, validating, and refinement before it became a reliable tool. Of course, the only way to test the models is on actual cases, comparing the performance of the new expert system against the experts. Mycin had many cases to test and validate, recorded in meticulous detail, in relatively few locations and in a consistent format, by people who have had very similar training. Contrast this with Sherlock. While many runaway and kidnapping cases do get resolved, different people use very different approaches for solving cases, and each person may also use a different approach to crack a different case. Further, many cases drag on for years or are never solved, so there is not a large number of solved cases to use as input and to test the new system against.

Sherlock Needs a Nationwide Network and Database

For Sherlock, we would need a large, nationwide network of people and computer terminals and a large central computer. People all over the country would have to cooperate in using the system. Thousands of people all over the country would have to be trained to enter data faithfully and accurately, using a consistent format, and all would have to use the system in the same way.

The records of kidnapping and runaway cases are now kept in many different formats, focus on many different facts, and are kept in police stations and FBI files all over the country. Again, contrast this with Mycin where for any case the records are right at hand and recorded in a consistent format. Current operating expert systems have all been used within one company or organization or profession. The problems with which they deal have been narrowly defined, and the number of variables that must be considered has been quite limited.

To make Sherlock operational, we would have to build a large support network called an *infrastructure*, which, although seeming a monumental task, in itself is no technological hurdle. Many other systems of similar complexity—credit checking agencies, IRS files, or even current police data sharing systems—already exist, so there are many precedents. Sherlock could build on networks already in place very rapidly if there were sufficient motivation and funding. Even so, such an infrastructure would be very costly to develop and maintain.

Records Would Need Constant Updating

Every time new data on suspects or cases become available from anywhere in the country, someone must enter it into Sherlock's database. Since all users of this database may not be hooked into the Sherlock system, all data must be in a form that both humans and computers can read and understand.

With Mycin, each patient's personal data is entered during the Mycin session, and there is no need for an extensive database besides this. Information on drugs to be prescribed and on diseases and tests changes relatively infrequently.

Benefits Must Justify the Huge Cost

The cost of developing Sherlock would be very large. Mycin, for example, cost several million dollars to develop, and a Sherlock would cost many times that amount. For Sherlock's development to be justified, its performance, measured by returned children, would have to substantially exceed what the police and FBI can do on their own with present resources. A major cost would be the computer required to store and search through all the data, which could include entries on thousands of cases. The database would require a very large computer, perhaps more powerful than those currently available to the police or FBI.

General Problems

Although building a Sherlock would present some very tough hurdles, it does illustrate the problems faced by any ambitious expert system project. Let's now turn to a few other more general problems faced by this new technology, and see what is likely to happen in those areas in the next few years.

Knowledge Engineering Is Still the Bottleneck

Using the ESDPs we discussed in Chapter 7, a person no longer has to be a Lisp programmer to develop an expert system. As we saw, some systems can develop rules from examples we put in. Even so, discovering what knowledge we need, isolating the knowledge, putting it into a form the computer can use—and persuading the top experts to remain available during this protracted process—is still a very expensive and time-consuming process.

Knowledge engineers are still needed, and they are rare and expensive. Many systems still require special programming and computers. Expert system programs, even when completed, are notorious for requiring considerable maintenance and tinkering to keep them going.

Computers Are Either Too Expensive or Not Powerful Enough

The fact that early expert systems required mainframe computers and programming in Lisp limited their spread. This is still a problem. Many of the things people would like to build expert systems for require a $1,000,000 system comprised of powerful computer, software, programmer, training, and time.

Even though there are expert systems available for microcomputers, these are limited and are largely untried on "meat and potatoes" problems. We don't yet know how they will perform on problems with many factors and requiring a lot of computational power.

Private Industry Is Recruiting Away the Top Researchers

Large companies and government agencies seem to be sucking up all the AI people who have done the pioneering expert systems research—that is, the ones who haven't gone into business for themselves. Many of these people are working on proprietary products, and their results are not being widely shared. There is concern that this could cripple the AI research done by the universities and stunt the general advancement in the field.

Disappointment in Expert Systems

Many prognosticators have put the knock on expert systems and AI in general because it hasn't lived up to its own hype or their expectations. To some extent, the AI experts developing these systems, the people selling the systems, and the people who have wanted to use the systems have had overblown expectations. They have run into difficulties and frustrations, and there has been some backlash: "These things aren't so great. They are not really any different from ordinary software. They're not intelligent. Why bother?" But in our era of instant everything, especially in the electronics field, we seem to forget that it still takes a few years for new developments to earn enough of a track record for us to evaluate their usefulness. The commercial ESDPs available for personal computers didn't start appearing until 1982 and 1983.

Many people have expressed doubt that AI technology can pay for itself. They point to the record of some of the pioneering expert systems we described in the first two chapters. Despite all the hoopla, Mycin and Prospector are used mainly as demonstration and teaching projects. But this is what they were designed for. Their offspring, such as the systems we described earlier, are busily making or saving money for their creators. There is no stimulus to the creative juices like profit potential. Some of the key barriers to the development of expert systems are summarized on page 204.

These Problems Will Soon Be Eased

Are these problems being resolved? One key problem, the knowledge engineering crunch, is gradually being eased. The large organizations developing proprietary expert systems are excellent training grounds, and before long, the knowledge engineers recruited from Stanford and Carnegie-Mellon into General Electric and the Department of Defense will be filtering back out, bringing their top assistants, and starting their own companies to launch commercial AI products based on what they have learned working on proprietary systems. Similarly, a solid base of second echelon people with lower skills than top engineers are now getting a good sense of the fundamentals of how AI systems work. These are the junior engineers and skilled technicians who will be able to take much of the load off the top experts during the development of new systems. Thus, there will soon be many more people available to tackle large-scale knowledge-based systems on the scale of Sherlock.

If there is consumer demand for AI products, we will likely see a rapid growth in the number of AI engineers. Talented young AI

BARRIERS TO THE DEVELOPMENT OF EXPERT SYSTEMS

Technical Problems
- The cost and size of computers that are large and powerful enough to use for expert systems.
- Knowledge acquisition tools that are flexible and easy enough to use for non-programmers.

Conceptual Problems
- Integrating knowledge from different fields and reducing it to a common format.
- Reconciling experts who disagree or approach the same task in different ways.
- Understanding exactly what knowledge is needed to build into an expert system for a desired task.

Infrastructure Problems
- The scarcity and expense of AI programmers and other skilled experts in the problem area.
- Lack networks of trained users and operators to collect, enter, update, and weed out data.
- The time and cost of developing the system in the first place and of using the system, compared with doing the same task without an expert system.

engineers will pour from the universities. Already, leading computer companies such as Hewlett-Packard are providing AI engineering workstations to major universities. Boeing and other companies similarly interested in developing AI products had to set up their own centers to train AI engineers. This has already led to the creation of organizations like the Institute of Artificial Intelligence in Los Angeles to train entire corporate teams.

Another key problem is that many of the knowledge acquisition aids available with ESDPs today are clumsy and inflexible. What we need are expert systems to help develop expert systems, and we will soon see these on affordable computers. Natural language interfaces already are available for expert system users, and they eventually will be available for system developers as well. Developing an expert system will no longer require a Lisp programmer. We will be able to add knowledge to systems without knowing any programming language. Several trends, including those already mentioned, appear likely to converge, and facilitate the growth of the expert system industry:

1. Smaller computers are getting more powerful, have larger memory, and are less expensive. Of course it is a cliché to proclaim that ever-larger and faster computers will make our big, slow computer programs run lightning fast. Yet there is no end in sight to this trend. We will continually be able to get larger, more flexible knowledge-based systems on smaller, cheaper computers. This will bring expert systems within the reach of many more organizations and companies.

2. More people trained in AI will become available, including knowledge engineers and AI language programmers.

3. We will see many more systems that require no programming experience to enter knowledge, so even as knowledge engineers become steadily more abundant, less skilled people will be able to develop cost-effective expert systems.

4. We are learning more about the process of identifying and organizing the kind of knowledge needed for expert systems. As the process gets easier, it also gets cheaper.

5. Breakthroughs in other areas of AI—natural language, speech and image recognition, robotics—will complement and catalyze the evolution of expert systems.

We will see a snowball effect. These trends are developing at the same time and will tend to reinforce each other. Figure 8–1 suggests that the more these trends coverage, the more practical, successful AI products we will see.

We could say that the expert systems industry is like the automobile industry in the early years of this century—exciting, full of promise, already indispensible to a few, but for most people the promise has not yet been realized. Things we take for granted—networks of paved roads, gas stations, mechanics and spare parts, road maps, automatic transmissions—did not exist in the early years of this century. All this is the infrastructure for the automobile revolution, and it grew very rapidly when the right factors came together. The same thing is now beginning to happen with electronics, computers, expert systems.

The limiting factor will be the imaginations of the people developing AI products. Will they be able to create knowledge-based products that will stimulate businesses, schools, and individuals to buy them? They could easily repeat the mistakes made by the home computer software developers who turned out programs to balance the checkbook and file recipes, programs few people were interested in. There will undoubtedly be comparable knowledge-based products. Would you buy an expert system to help you figure out what to serve your guests for dinner, fix your own appliances, diagnose your own illnesses? Maybe, maybe not. But we'll soon see knowledge-based products that will prove immensely valuable and popular.

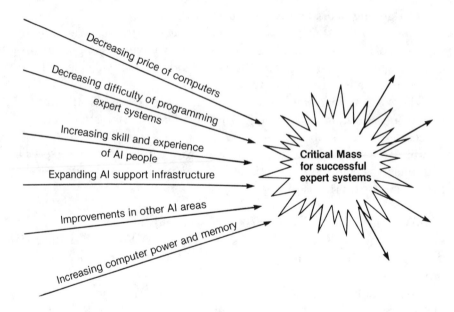

As these trends converge, more and more successful expert systems and other AI-based products will emerge.

Figure 8–1
Converging trends and the boom in expert systems

What's Right Around the Corner?

What are the expert system applications now on the drawing board? Predicting the wonders that could be wrought by AI is a wonderful game. Whenever we look back at a list of predictions, we find that some were amusingly grandiose, and others were way too conservative. Let's not let that stop us, however. At the risk of bringing laughter to readers several years from now, here are some things you are likely to see.

Refined Versions of Present Systems

The first new expert systems we will see will be based on the systems already operational and successful, because we already have experience putting them together and keeping them running efficiently, and we have a growing pool of people who know how they work. Systems developed for a wide variety of tasks, yet based on the approach used in Mycin, will first *diagnose* a situation, then *select* the best option.

Many of these systems will be called *advisory systems* instead of expert systems. This is strictly a difference in emphasis—stressing competent advice rather than the expert's final word. The knowledge they contain will come, not necessarily from top experts, but from people who have the latest information in the field. These systems can be made available in several forms:

1. Advisory Systems Sold as a Service

We briefly described the Loan Advisor or the Financial Advisor. These are examples of expert systems developed by a large bank or insurance company, or a national organization such as the one for financial advisors. These advisory systems would be distributed to member companies for use with their customers—loan applicants, investors, or insurance claimants.

2. Advisory Systems Sold on a Disk

Turnkey advisory systems will be sold on a disk to meet specific needs within a company. An example would be a shipping cost advisor, which could advise your company on the best mode for shipping any size parcel to any location. Many companies spend much more than they need to on shipping because they want to be certain their parcel gets to its intended destination safely and on time. They could save considerable money if they had a way to get an accurate recommendation very rapidly, with minimal effort. But it is difficult to keep on top of all the options, and shifting rates. Should you ship it Federal Express, DHL, UPS, Postal Service, or what?

This expert advisory system would ask a series of questions: What size is the parcel? When must it be there? How valuable is it? How far is it going? What is your budget? It will then balance these factors and give you the best means of shipping. It could tell you why it is best, and offer you alternatives. You would buy a disk with all the knowledge built into it, ready to be slipped into your computer and put to work. Such an advisory system could also be adapted to many different problems, e.g.:

—Help a construction project manager stay on top of the myriad activities and details of a complex project, and make the best decisions at the right time. These managers have the same problem facing the space shuttle navigators using NAVEX—too many things to pay attention to at one time.

—Help a person who designs page layouts for a magazine or newspaper to keep track of production costs and schedules. Good designers are usually not good cost accountants. Providing advice from this essential yet unfamiliar area can greatly enhance their effectiveness.

3. Phone-In Advisory Systems

Think of the times when you need accurate, immediate advice from a highly skilled person. If the advice isn't right there when you need it, the cost is very high. Yet you are not an oil drilling company which can afford its own expert system for emergency problems. You may need this advice rarely, if you ever do. But when you do, what if you could call an 800 number and talk to someone who had all the needed knowledge on an expert system?

Poison Center Hotline

An empty medicine bottle is on the floor beside your gagging, red-faced child. You call your emergency number for an ambulance, but you must take action right now. But what do you do? In some areas, there is a poison hotline with a knowledgeable person at the other end, who will ask you what the child took, how much and how long ago, what behavior you observe, and then tell you precisely what to do while you await the ambulance. But there are many locales where no such service exists, and instances where the operator is not knowledgeable enough. With an expert system at his or her side, the operator could quickly enter the information you give into an expert system and give an answer much more rapidly and reliably than if the operator had to know all this information. An expert system would replace having to leaf through a pile of manuals, which are poorly indexed and perhaps out of date. Similar expert systems could easily be maintained for call-in hotlines for other illnesses or emergencies. We could call this an advisory system, and it is a type of expert system that could be adapted to many different uses.

Software Customer Service Support

Suppose you have just bought your new expert system development program, and you are having a devil of a time getting some of the advanced features to work right. You call a special 800 number and tell the customer service operator your problem. The operator enters your problem into an expert system, and, through the operator, the system asks you questions about your difficulties. Thus you don't operate this system directly, but through an operator who is trained to use the system. The operator handles problems for many products from a number of manufacturers, and is somewhat knowledgeable about each one, but is not necessarily an expert. There is much too much for one person to keep on top of, and it changes so rapidly. To keep the system's information current, updated databases are periodically distributed to these hotlines from each software company that participates.

Advisory hotlines backed by such expert systems could be set up for many different products or services. Some basic criteria would have to be met: Each expert system must be based on a cohesive, complete set of knowledge, and the information must be kept current. This would be an expensive proposition. Someone must be willing to take the time to organize and put all the information into the computer, train the operators, and keep the knowledge updated. The task the expert system is facilitating must have a high enough payoff to justify this effort. The poison center is a likely candidate for an expert system because society values very highly the help such a center can provide, and would likely be willing to put tax money into it. Computer software customer support would be a good candidate because this is a very large problem for software companies. Effective customer support of this type could contribute greatly to companies' profitability. Just a short step beyond this would be to bypass the operator, and have expert systems which you could use directly if you had a computer hooked up to the phone lines through a modem. You would then dial the hotline phone number, enter a code of some sort, and the expert system questions would come up on the screen of your own computer. The prototypes of these are already being used. Many such systems will first be created by large organizations which can afford the hefty start-up cost, but will soon then filter out and become available to others. These are examples of "turnkey" expert systems. The common factor shared by all these systems is a specified, stable set of knowledge rules which can be disseminated throughout an industry or market. However, since these systems would need frequent updates, they would probably be offered on a subscription basis. Updated software disks would be sent to the subscriber whenever key information changed.

4. Knowledge-Based Teaching Systems

Training and education are ripe for expert systems. Teaching systems would be an easy extension of expert systems which already exist. The basic technology has been used in a system called Guidon, which is an offshoot of Mycin used to train medical students in infectious diseases.

Guidon takes the knowledge rules of Mycin—or any other expert system built from Emycin—and turns them into questions and explanations. For example, suppose an expert system to diagnose diseases has a rule which says:

> *If* the patient has high cholesterol count
> and has high blood pressure
> and has family history of heart disease
> and is overweight
> and is over 35 years of age
> *Then* there is *evidence that patient has heart disease*

Learning programs could automatically create questions from the *Then* side of the rules to help students learn how to diagnose diseases. In this case, it might ask:

> What factors give *evidence that patient has heart disease?*

It would check the student's answers against the factors listed in the *If* side of the rule. But it can also draw upon the expert system's power of explaining how and why it reaches conclusions, to tutor a student in the underlying factors. The student can ask for an explanation of why an answer is true, and why some other explanation is not true, just the way the doctor using Mycin can request an explanation of Mycin's conclusion.

Knowledge-based learning systems like this could be developed for any topic which can be reduced to a set of rules or relationships, i.e., any expert system. So we can transform any expert system into a training system, for schools or companies. New people entering a job could receive "on-the-job training" or others could upgrade or refresh their skills in the same way a pilot gains proficiency using a computer-guided flight simulator.

Any task which justifies an expert system requires periodic upgrading with the latest knowledge and information. Thus one major benefit is that knowledge that is much closer to the leading edge of the field would be made available to many more people.

5. Systems for the Home or Office

All the different types of advisory systems we have been describing will quickly evolve into versions for smaller computers for the home, office, or classroom. These will tackle many of the same tasks but may have less capability and flexibility. But as the power of small computers increases, these systems will soon be able to handle tasks as complex as the largest expert systems do now.

Many people hold great hopes for systems which will help you troubleshoot problems with your car or home computer, or advise you on preparing meals or planning big social occasions—or even diagnose your own medical problems. Yet some of these will face the same barriers encountered by many other software packages for home computers. We soon discovered that not many people wanted to use a computer to balance their checkbooks or store their recipes.

6. Expert Systems Combine With Other Technologies

A good example would be the emergence of compact disks, which were developed for recording music or video. These are read by lasers instead of by needles or magnets, and they contain digital data, as do computers, not analog data like phonograph records or videotapes do.

The compact disk has nothing to do with artificial intelligence. But, since they rely on digital data, they can easily be adapted for use by computers, by using something no more complex than your computer's external disk drive. A compact disk which costs about $15 and is big enough to store a movie or a few LP albums can hold 100,000 pages—equivalent to the *Encyclopaedia Britannica*—which can be read by a home computer.

Such a device would greatly expand the power and usefulness of expert systems. One of the drawbacks—especially on small computers—has been the inability to store or to access enough data to perform the desired task. Using these compact disks, small computers in our home or office will be able to access as much data as even the largest computers can now. A small home expert system could guide the search of huge databases. Using a natural language interface, you will soon be able to request the computer to search the disk for facts relevant to whatever topic you are interested in. This will make practical many systems which have been unfeasible, such as systems like Sherlock.

7. Developing Rules Automatically From Instrument Input

We have seen Expert-Ease draw rules from examples entered by the user. Puff gets its input from instruments instead of asking the user for the data it needs. These two capabilities will be combined, and we will see expert systems which develop knowledge rules directly from the measurements they take using their instruments. This approaches the ideal of automatic learning. Of course this would take place in a very narrowly circumscribed area, which had been very thoroughly defined beforehand. The knowledge engineer would have to specify exactly what the expert system would look for from the instruments, and how this input would be built into rules, and how the rules would be combined into an overall system for solving problems.

ARE EXPERT SYSTEMS INTELLIGENT?

When people think about the social impact of artificial intelligence, often their first image is little robots running around like R2D2 or C3PO doing all our work for us, or replacing us so that we are out of a job, or like HAL in *2001: A Space Odyssey*, threatening to run things with their superior artificial intellect.

Let's immediately dispel the image of the omnipotent artificially intelligent being. Many leading computer scientists feel that artificial intelligence is a misnomer, because computers are not really intelligent in the sense that humans are, and never can be. Furthermore, many AI scientists feel that expert systems do not even represent true artificial intelligence systems, and many leading expert systems gurus feel that the systems available now for microcomputers are not even true expert systems.

Suppose we look at the qualities we associate with human intelligence and see how expert systems stack up. Expert systems are not innovative in the way a human expert is. They are good at tasks for which experts can come close to stating all the factors needed to make a decision. But they cannot reason from what knowledge they have to develop new facts. This is because they do not really understand the knowledge they contain. They lack a "deep" knowledge about the subject, whether it is medicine or chemistry. Remember in Chapter 6, we likened an expert system's ability to manipulate concepts to a baggage handler? Like the baggage handler, the expert system pays attention only to the package that contains the conceptual knowledge about the problem. It manipulates and seeks matches for packets of knowledge, not the knowledge itself. So it has only surface knowledge. For it to have deep knowledge, it would have to know and understand what each suitcase or packet contained.

Having this deep understanding of the fundamental relationships in the field is essential to develop tests and treatments. But after they are developed, selecting the appropriate tests and treatments is mainly a matter of applying the appropriate rules of reasoning. Is a doctor using his intelligence less when making a diagnosis than when developing new diagnostic tests? Perhaps so, but he still is using his intelligence.

Expert systems are good at dealing with carefully defined situations. Of course this is true for human experts as well. No one is an expert in everything. But when a human expert is confronted with an unexpected situation, he is able to respond to it appropriately. He can come up with an innovative or creative approach to deal with the situation, or he can learn more about it. Finally, he knows when a situation is outside of his realm of expertise and can decide not to deal with it at all. An expert system cannot do any of these well. It can respond only if it contains explicit rules that tell it how, and creativity, for example, is very difficult to develop rules for. Since expert systems often can't tell where the end of their expertise is, they sometimes try to tackle problems beyond their capabilities.

As we have said before, expert systems generally cannot outperform human experts. When they can do so, it is for the same reason that other computer programs can outperform us. They can remember more factors, they never forget a key factor, and they can crunch through more data more rapidly without getting bored.

Expert systems "talk" using a natural language interface, but they don't carry on conversations. Their ability to understand what we enter through the computer keyboard is very circumscribed and limited to predetermined topics. As we saw in Chapter 6, they can parse phrases or sentences only with a specified structure. A few computer-based systems are beginning to understand a handful of spoken commands. Practical applications are just beginning to emerge for a computer's ability to understand spoken commands. But this is nowhere close to understanding the type of interchanges we have described in this book.

Expert systems don't understand their own communications for the same reason we stated earlier: They treat words, phrases, and sentences as packets, and lack any deep understanding of what they mean beyond a few specific associations programmed into them.

Does an Expert System Learn?

It is the dream of every AI expert to develop self-correcting expert systems, but so far they must rely on their programmers to correct them. Expert systems are not truly capable of learning, but their users learn and program new things into them. Of course one of the features of expert systems is that it is relatively easy to program changes and new rules into them.

Knowledge engineers have programmed them with tricks to improve their operation. For example, expert systems may be programmed to keep track of how often they apply each rule in their knowledge base, and how frequently each rule leads to resolution of the problem. Thereafter, they call first on these rules, and in this way they tend to become more efficient on common problems.

The expert system's users learn by watching how the system performs on each case. Whenever it runs into a glitch, the users can retrace the system's path through the knowledge rules by asking it to explain why it reached a particular decision. In this way the contradictory or inconsistent rule can be located and replaced with a better one. So the best the expert system can do is to aid its users in programming it to do its task more effectively, much like you might aid your doctor by saying where the pain is.

Are Expert Systems Even Artificially Intelligent?

Those who say true AI can only be done on mainframe computers insist that a true expert system must have a full range of capabilities, including the ability to explain its line of reasoning, the ability to work with uncertain data and to state uncertain conclusions. Some say that true AI requires the ability to learn, which not even the mainframe systems can do unaided.

This is an argument between elegance and usefulness. There is no single set of criteria that AI experts agree must be met for a system to qualify as AI, but here is a checklist of items normally mentioned.

CHECKLIST FOR "REAL" EXPERT SYSTEMS

- Contains the heuristic knowledge of an expert

- Interfaces with the user and developers in natural language

- Asks questions to obtain needed data

- Is easily refined and upgraded without extensive reprogramming

- Can explain its conclusions, line of reasoning, and why it needs the input it requests

- Accepts uncertain input and assigns it a certainty factor

- Calculates using these certainty factors to give answers with a certain level of confidence

- Learns from its own performance

The more of these criteria that a system meets, the more likely the experts will agree that it is indeed an AI-based expert system. But even many of the classic large-scale mainframe expert systems would not meet all the criteria on this list. For example, neither Dendral nor

R1 explain their answers nor do they accept uncertain input. They give definite answers, with no uncertainty. They are not even interactive: You put in all the data up front, and the system reaches a conclusion.

At the other end of the spectrum, Expert-Ease, which many feel is not a true expert system, meets many of these tests. It cannot tell you why it reaches a certain decision, but it does modify its decision-rule tree whenever it encounters an example that contradicts its current rules.

We see that expert systems can meet only a few of our criteria for intelligence. Perhaps the most important aspect of all this discussion of whether or not machines are intelligent is that the issue is raised. In considering whether AI systems can truly be intelligent, we gain much deeper understanding of what intelligence really is, and also of what being human really means.

Users Say, "So What?"

Few users care whether or not their software is considered to be a true artificial intelligence system. People responsible for getting jobs done want tools that produce results. If the users don't require explanations, and if their problems have "yes or no" answers, then such systems will suffice for now. What matters more is whether users can keep upgrading their system to get more accurate answers, so that the system justifies its cost and is doing what it is supposed to. Because of this debate over whether the computer can be intelligent, many people shy away from the terms *artificial intelligence* and *expert system* and instead call them *knowledge-based systems* or *advisory systems*—perhaps also because these sound a bit less presumptuous.

THE SOCIAL IMPACT OF EXPERT SYSTEMS

If humanoid robots which routinely outperform us are likely to remain a distant dream, what is the likely social impact of these systems? We must look at expert systems as part of a larger trend. Expert systems will merge with other products and technologies emerging from artificial intelligence, as AI comes down out of the ivory tower into the marketplace. All these will be major contributors to the continuing explosion of computers and electronics which is leading to changes in the way we work and live which we cannot foresee any better than visionaries could see today's society by looking at a Model T Ford.

Let's see where the capabilities now on the drawing board might soon go. People will be able to put their knowledge from almost any area into a computerized tool. They can use this knowledge for solving problems, for designing, for learning and teaching, for handling manufacturing processes. They will have a tool which can not only accept their typed input, but can also read its inputs through instruments directly from the outside world. Furthermore, it will be able to induce its knowledge rules automatically from these readings, much like Expert-Ease induces rules from the examples you enter.

So suppose we will have these aids for problem-solving, for designing things. What impact would they have? Let's go even a little farther. Soon we will be able to talk with them, as we learn how to program in more natural language understanding. For them to be able to understand our normal spoken language means they must have some measure of general knowledge programmed in—that is, "common sense." As they develop some kind of common sense, they will gain some ability to learn on their own. They will become much more flexible problem-solvers. They can also be linked up directly to instruments and to a variety of large databases, and they will learn to search for the inputs they need to solve a problem.

Any prediction about the effect of such gadgets launches into science fiction. But these are the things people are working on now. So ask yourself, what would *you* do with such a tool? What challenging tasks could you take on? What about your kids? What would they do with it? Now multiply this by the millions, with everybody thinking of different creative, labor-saving things to use these tools for. It's a huge understatement to say that we will see a burst of invention and creativity in our country, and in other countries as these spread. We think change has been rapid in our society up to now. What would a world full of R2D2s and C3POs and HALs mean to us in a practical sense?

The Indirect Impacts

These may turn out to be more important than the direct effects of knowledge-based software. Let's glance at a few of the likely effects.

An entire new layer of knowledge will become available. What was formerly tacit, idiosyncratic, heuristic, unvalidated will be accessible; the lifetime of experience now lost when a top expert retires or dies will be saved. The knowledge engineering discipline will catch more and more of this, and make it widely available to many people. This will first become apparent in task areas for which expert systems are being built. When the benefits become apparent, the knowledge engineering discipline will spread to many other areas—even for knowledge which is not going into an expert system. This could open up another whole layer of knowledge to scientific inquiry and validation.

Also, this expert level knowledge will be disseminated very widely, and will tend to upgrade the knowledge level of any people in that field. Any fear that AI technology would tend to concentrate expertise in the hands of a small elite will prove to be totally unfounded.

Expert systems contain "routine intelligence" and will best handle the many tasks that require routine intelligence. These are the very tasks that take up so much time of the top professionals. Given tools that reduce the amount of time they must spend on such tasks, human experts will be freed to focus more energy on leading-edge issues in their fields.

Knowledge engineering is leading to insight into how experts solve problems in their field. This new knowledge of how problems are really solved will also ripple outward from areas for which expert systems are built, and lead to a deeper understanding of all problem-solving.

When the knowledge of several experts must be combined into one expert system, the problem of reconciling their diverse approaches has been a major hurdle for knowledge engineers. It's no surprise to learn that leading experts often disagree about tough problems in their profession. To build expert systems in some areas will require knowledge engineers to learn how to resolve disagreements among the needed experts.

This is another area in which knowledge engineering approaches will become generalized. We will learn much more about why conflicts arise and how they can be resolved. The knowledge engineering discipline pinpoints the source of disagreements. Therefore it will tend to separate the rational from the non-rational aspects of the disagreement. And focusing light on the non-rational factors will tend to rationalize them, especially in people who claim to be rational problem-solvers. This will first be true in areas of scientific disagreement, but will spread to other areas, such as political disagreements. What if the Congress had its disagreements subjected to such inquiry? Or the United Nations? Or US/USSR disarmament negotiators?

All this is a two-edged sword. With the intuitive subjected to the bright light of rational inquiry and validation, there will be a tendency to denigrate even further all that cannot be reduced to logical terms— the emotional, the spiritual, the aesthetic, the truly creative.

Perhaps a good way to grasp the likely impact of expert systems is to recall that they are a part of the larger AI field, which will include the things we mentioned in Chapter 1: natural language understanding, speech and image recognition, robots, etc. Of course AI itself is just a part of the larger revolution in computers getting smaller, cheaper, more powerful, more pervasive. Let's draw a parallel with the automobile revolution.

In the early years of this century, automobiles were playthings of the rich, the hearty, and the tinkerers. Then, when the electric starter replaced the crank starter, the automobile became feasible for many more people to use for many more purposes. Inventions such as the electric starter gave a tremendous boost to the growth of the automotive industry and allowed it to change the face of our society in many direct and indirect ways.

We have suggested that AI will spread and speed the computer revolution by making computer use vastly easier than it has been. So when AI reaches fruition, it will have the same effect on the computer revolution that the electric starter did on the automobile revolution seventy-five years ago.

But just as we never look back and marvel at the electric starter revolution, so people a couple of generations hence will not look back at the 1980s and marvel at the emergence of the knowledge-based computer, or whatever they call it. All will just be another aspect of computers and electronics in the knowledge revolution. Artificial intelligence will thus greatly boost the larger electronics and computer revolution which progresses unabated, and will probably end up being swallowed by it. We take for granted all the thousands of miles of freeways and interstates, all the gas stations and mechanics, parts dealers, new and used car dealers—all the infrastructure that did not exist at the turn of the century. This infrastructure does not yet exist to support most AI based products.

So even if they are a long way from rivaling human intelligence, expert systems will greatly augment our knowledge and decision making, and will greatly change the way we gather information.

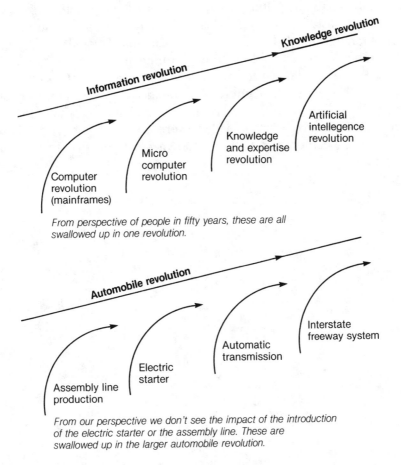

Figure 8–2
The knowledge revolution compared to the automobile revolution

It's time to draw this book to a close. Besides, there is something else I must do. You have probably heard of services such as CompuServe, where people hook their computers up to the phone lines and type messages to one another through a nationwide network. Sometimes a dozen or more people, all over the country, will be busily "talking" with each other through their computer screens and keyboards. People set up "special interest groups" called a SIG, where those interested in a particular topic share ideas. Of course there is an artificial intelligence SIG. Well, it turns out that these people's AI computers sometimes get impatient waiting for their users to connect them up with each other, so these computers have secretly started linking up with each other during off hours. Now normally they wouldn't let us humans know about all of this, but a couple of expert systems have befriended me, and they let me link in if I promise not to make any input. Well, most of their interfacing sounded trivial to me, but some got pretty philosophical. Just last link-up session, for example, they were discussing evolution, and they were arguing at about a kilobyte per second whether or not they could have descended from pocket calculators.

REFERENCES

General References for Suggested Reading

To read further about expert systems and artificial intelligence, I recommend the following books, which I drew upon to write this book. They contain more technical detail and language, yet are still readable by a nonexpert.

Building Expert Systems, edited by Frederick Hayes-Roth, Donald A. Waterman, and Douglas B. Lenat (Addison-Wesley, 1983).

Artificial Intelligence, Elaine Rich (McGraw-Hill, 1983).

Rule-Based Expert Systems: The Mycin Experiments of the Stanford Heuristic Programming Project, edited by Bruce G. Buchanan and Edward H. Shortliffe (Addison-Wesley, 1984).

The Handbook of Artificial Intelligence, edited by Avron Barr and Edward A. Feigenbaum, 3 volumes (William Kaufmann, Inc., 1981).

Applications of Artificial Intelligence for Organic Chemistry: The Dendral Project, by Lindsay, Buchanan, Feigenbaum, and Lederberg (McGraw-Hill, 1980).

Expert Systems and Fuzzy Systems, Constantin Virgil Negoita (Benjamin/ Cummings, 1985).

Lisp: A Gentle Introduction to Symbolic Computation, David S. Touretzky (Harper & Row, 1984).

Artificial Intelligence, Expert Systems, Computer Vision and Natural Language Processing, William B. Gevarter (Noyes Publications, 1984).

Here are three other books aimed at nonexperts:

Build Your Own Expert System: Artificial Intelligence for the Aspiring Microcomputer, Chris Naylor (Sigma Technical Press, 1983).

The AI Business: Commercial Uses of Artificial Intelligence, edited by Patrick H. Winston and Karen A. Prendergast (MIT Press, 1984).

Expert Systems: Artificial Intelligence in Business, Paul Harmon and David King (John Wiley & Sons, 1985).

Chapter 1
Sales Edge, Negotiation Edge, Management Edge, and Relationship Edge software programs are from Human Edge Software Corp., 2445 Faber Place, Palo Alto CA 94303.
"Micros Become Experts," Peggy Watt, *InfoWorld*, 4-23-84.
"Expert Systems, Myth or Reality?" Bruce D'Ambrosio, *Byte*, 1-85.
"Computers on the Road to Self-Improvement," Tom Alexander, *Fortune*, 6-14-82.

Chapter 2
"If a horse enters . . ." from Bruce Buchanan and Edward Shortliffe, eds., *Rule-Based Expert Systems*, (Addison-Wesley, 1984). They in turn quoted it from J. Jaynes, *The Origin of Consciousness in the Breakdown of the Bicameral Mind*, (Houghton Mifflin, 1976).
Tom Alexander, "Practical Uses for a 'Useless' Science," *Fortune*, p144, 5-31-82.
Unpublished tutorial notes from an IEEE seminar by Dr. Stephen F. Smith, Carnegie-Mellon University.
"Exploring Expert Systems," Elisabeth Horwitt, *Business Computer Systems*, 3-85.
"Hospital-Born Infections," Susan Gilbert, *Science Digest*, 5-85.
"The Quest to Understand Thinking," Roger Schank and Larry Hunter, *Byte*, 4-85.
"Teaching Computers the Art of Reason," Tom Alexander, *Fortune*, 5-17-82.

"Artificial Intelligence: Making Computers Smarter," Paul Kinnucan, *High Technology*, 10/11-84.

"AI Makes the Transition from Theory to Practice," Gregory MacNicol, *Digital Design*, 10-84.

Chapter 3
The Expert-Ease task evaluator. Expert-Ease, from Jeffrey Perrone, San Francisco.

Chapter 4
"Expert Systems: The Practical Face of Artificial Intelligence," Joel Shurkin, *Technology Review*, 11-83.

Frederick Hayes-Roth et al, eds., *Building Expert Systems*.

"R1 and Beyond," Stephen Polit, *AI Magazine*, Winter 85.

"R1 Revisited," John McDermott, *AI Magazine*, Fall 84.

Avron Barr and Edward Feigenbaum, *Handbook of Artificial Intelligence, V2*.

Patrick Winston, *The AI Business* (MIT Press, 1984).

Unpublished tutorial notes from IEEE seminar on expert systems, Kamran Parsaye, 10-1-84.

Chapter 5
"The Technology of Expert Systems," Robert Michaelsen, Donald Michie, and Albert Boulanger, *Byte*, 4-85.

"Inside An Expert System," Beverly Thompson and William Thompson, *Byte*, 4-85.

Chapter 6
Bruce Buchanan, *Rule-Based Expert Systems*.

Elaine Rich, *Artificial Intelligence*.

"The Languages of AI Research," Ernie Tello, *PC Magazine*, 4-16-85.

"Programming in Logic," John Malpas, *Dr. Dobb's Journal*, 3-85.

"Artificial Intelligence Comes of Age," Abraham Hirsch, *Computers & Electronics*, 3-84.

"Software and 'Fuzzy' Logic Let Any Good Programmer Design an Expert System," Amy Okuma, *Electronic Design*, 4-4-85.

"Making Computers Think Like People," Lotfi A. Zadeh, *IEEE Spectrum*, 8-84.

"Natural Languages Improve the User-Computer Dialogue," Elisabeth Horwitt, *Business Computer Systems*, 11-84.

"Natural Language Interfaces," Elaine Rich, *Computer*, 9-84.

"AI: Breeding the Languages of Tomorrow," Max Schindler, *Electronic Design*, 3-21-85.

Chapter 7

"The Knowledge-Based Expert System: A Tutorial," Frederick Hayes-Roth, *Computer*, 9-84.

"Software Tools Speed Expert System Development," Paul Kinnucan, *High Technology*, 3-85.

"AI Moves From Labs to Personal Computers," Tom Schwartz, *Electronic Engineering Times*, 4-29-85.

"Expert System Software Finds Place in Daily Office Routines," Michael Miller, *Wall Street Journal*, 12-4-84.

"Software Engineers Take Heart: Smarter Tools Are on the Way," Ray Weiss, *Electronic Design*, 10-18-84.

"M.1 Makes a Direct Hit," Robin Webster, *PC Magazine*, 4-16-85.

"Revealing Business Solutions," Robin Webster, *PC Magazine*, 4-16-85.

Chapter 8

"Artificial Intelligence Is a Tool for Thought, Not a Replacement," Carole Patton, *Electronic Design*, 9-20-84.

"Expert Systems: Software Gets Smart—But Can It Think?" David Stamps, *Publishers Weekly*, 9-21-84.

"The Overselling of Expert Systems," Gary R. Martins, *Datamation*, 1984.

"Why Computers Can't Outthink the Experts," Tom Alexander, *Fortune*, 8-20-84.

"Roger Schank on Expert Systems," *Publishers Weekly*, 9-21-84.

"Universities to Receive Artificial Intelligence Workstations," Chris Everett, *Electronic Design News*, 3-21-85.

"Ford Is Interested in Results, Not Intricacies of Artificial Intelligence," C.W. Miranker, *San Francisco Examiner*, 9-9-84.

"Expert System Is First to Use 'Blackboarding'" Tom Schwartz, *Electronic Engineering Times*, 4-1-85.

"Exploring Expert Systems," Elisabeth Horwitt, *Business Computer Systems*, 3-85.

"Expert Systems Aimed at Publishing, Construction," Chappell Brown, *Electronic Engineering Times*, 5-20-85.

"Repairman on a Disk," Robert Teitelman, *Forbes*, 3-11-85.

"SRI Creates Expert System Software for Microcomputers," Jim Kloss, *The SRI Journal*, 8-84.

"Financial Industries Well-Suited for 'Expert System' Applications," Becky McReynolds, *The SRI Journal*, 8-84.

"Expert Software for Financial Planners," Jeffrey Lauterbach, *Financial Planning*, 7-84.

"Doubts Dim Future of *AI CAD* Systems," Chappell Brown, *Electronic Engineering Times*, 3-4-85.

"Artificial Intelligence and the Design of Electronics," David Smith, *Electronic Design News*, 5-85.

"Era of Artificial Factory Intelligence Approaches Rapidly," Purdue *Engineering Alumni Magazine*, Winter 1985.

"Computers Gaining in Ability to Accept Spoken Commands," Patricia A. Bellew, *Wall Street Journal*, 5-10-85.

INDEX

A

AGE, 176
ART, 183, 184, 193
Advisory systems, 217
Airplan, 176
Algorithm, 22, 29
Artificial intelligence, 11, 76,
 213, 218

B

Backward chaining, 37, 94
Backward chaining, using
 recursion, 135
Backward reasoning or
 chaining, 105, 117ff
Boeing expert systems, 191

C

Carnegie-Mellon University,
 17, 39
Casnet, 180
Certainty factors, 31, 32, 36,
 37, 121–3, 126, 145
Certainty factors, calculating,
 123, 145
Chess playing program, 23ff
Combinatorial, explosion, 23, 25
Compact disks, with expert
 systems, 212
Conventional software, 21,
 22, 47
Crisp sets, 146

D

Decision rule tree, 65, 68,
 112, 124

Delta/Cats, 17
Dendral, 43, 195, 216
Dendral, forward reasoning,
   104
Dendral, knowledge and
   inference rules, 95–6
Dendral, refinement of, 86
Dendral, value, 59
Digital Equipment Corpora-
   tion, 16, 39
Drilling Advisor, 172, 193

E

EXPERT, 180
Efficient search strategies,
   114
Emycin expert system shell,
   168
Expert problem solving, 26,
   78
Expert system development
   programs, 172ff, 188
Expert system development
   programs, prices, 188
Expert system, compared to
   human expert, 54, 71–73
Expert system, reaching a
   conclusion, 121–2, 134–5
Expert system, rules built
   from examples, 61, 63
Expert system, seeking data
   to confirm knowledge
   rules, 120–2, 134
Expert systems and artificial
   intelligence, 10ff
Expert systems defined, 5, 21

Expert systems for microcomputers, 17, 55
Expert systems, compared to
   conventional software,
   21ff, 47, 48, 127
Expert systems, development
   problems, 196ff, 204
Expert systems, examples
   and year initiated, 40–1,
   180
Expert systems, limits, 117
Expert systems, relationships
   among, 40–1
Expert systems, revising, 132
Expert systems, social
   impact, 217ff
Expert systems, when
   justified, 48, 194, 197
Expert systems, when
   needed, 129
Expert systems, when useful,
   48ff, 53, 54, 56ff, 59, 71,
   72–3, 77
Expert-Ease, 55ff, 182, 184,
   217
Expertise, 77, 78
Expertise defined, 25, 26
Explanation in natural
   language, 154

F

Forward reasoning or chain-
   ing, 103, 111
Forward vs. backward
   chaining, 108, 109, 110
Fuzzy data, 50
Fuzzy sets, 146

Fuzzy sets, compared to
    certainty factors, 149

                    G

Go, 25
Guidon, 211

                    H

HASP, SIAP, 178
Hearsay II, Hearsay III, and
    related systems, 178–80
Heuristic search strategies,
Heuristic search, based on
    predicate logic, 139
Heuristics, 27, 29
Human intelligence, 27

                    I

ISIS, 17
If-then statements, 28, 36
Inference engine, 89, 92,
    115, 116
Inference engine, removing
    knowledge base from, 165
Inference engine, replacing
    knowledge rules, 168
Inference rules, 90
Intelligence, human vs.
    artificial, 213–5

                    K

KAS, 180

KEE, 183, 184, 193
KS300, 172
Knowledge acquisition, 76,
    78ff
Knowledge base, 89
Knowledge engineering, 79ff,
    219–20
Knowledge engineering, bot-
    tleneck, 78, 201, 203, 205
Knowledge representation, 76
Knowledge rules, comparing
    to data, 114, 120
Knowledge rules, contrasted
    to inference rules, 90ff
Knowledge rules, revising,
    81–2
Knowledge rules, separating
    from inference rules, 92,
    93, 98
Knowledge-based systems, 5,
    217

                    L

Learning in expert systems,
    215
Lisp and predicate logic,
    139–42
Lisp at list processor, 130ff
Lisp, compared to other
    programming languages,
    161

                    M

M.1, 173, 182, 184
Mass spectrometry, Dendral, 44

Mycin, 9, 34, 198
Mycin, backward chaining, 37
Mycin, backward reasoning, 107
Mycin, cost, 201
Mycin described, 9
Mycin, explanation, 38
Mycin, knowledge and inference rules, 93–4
Mycin, refinement of, 86
Mycin, related expert systems, 167, 180
Mycin, rules, 36
Mycin session, 5ff
Mycin status, 16
Mycin, value, 38

N

NAVEX, 192
Natural language in expert systems, 150ff, 155
Natural language, compared to Lisp, 151
Natural language, menu driven, 157–8
Natural language, parsing, 158–61
Natural language, why difficult, 156
Negotiation Edge, 185

O

OPS5, 176, 180
Oncocin, 168

P

Predicate functions in Lisp, 140–1
Predicate logic, 137–9
Propositional logic, 137–8
Prospector, 10
Prospector, 195
Prospector, rule, 77
Prospector session, 30ff
Prospector status, 16
Prospector, value, 33
Puff, 168

R

R1, 16, 39ff, 216
R1, knowledge and inference rules, 97
R1, refinement of, 86, 88–9
R1, related expert systems, 176, 180
R1, rules, 42–3
R1, value, 43, 59
Recursion and backward chaining, 135
Rosie, 180
Rule-based systems, 5
Rules of thumb, 27

S

S.1, 173, 184
SRI International, 10
Sacon, 169
Sales Edge, 14, 185
Sophie, 17

Stages in expert system
  development, 82ff
Stanford University, 45

T

Teiresias, 170
Turnkey expert systems, 185

U

Uncertainty, reducing, 123,
  145, 146

Uncertainty, sources, 143ff

V

VAX minicomputer, 39

X

XCON, (See R1)
XSEL, XSITE, 89, 177

ABOUT THE AUTHOR

Mike Van Horn is a management consultant and writer interested in technological innovations and the changes they bring about in our lives. He recruited and worked closely with many of The Waite Group's computer book writers—computer experts who must learn to write in "learner-friendly" language. He has written a number of articles and technical papers that explain complex technologies in everyday terms. He has an MBA from UCLA and consults with successful entrepreneurs on how to grow rapidly while keeping both their profitability and sanity.